*Foolhardy*

# Personal Story Publishing Project Series

***Bearing Up***, 2018
- making do, bearing up, and overcoming adversity

***Exploring***, 2019
- discoveries, challenges, and adventures

***That Southern Thing***, 2020
- living, loving, laughing, loathing, leaving the South

***Luck and Opportunity***, sping 2021
- between if and if only

***Trouble***, fall 2021
- causing, avoiding, getting in, and getting out

***Curious Stuff***, spring 2022
- mementos, treasures, white elephants, and junk

***Twists and Turns***, fall 2022
- inflection points in life by choice, happenstance, misfortune, failure, and grace

***Lost & Found***, spring 2023
- loss and discovery—trials, serendipity, and life after

***Sooner or Later***, fall 2023
- about time, timing, and inevitability

***Now or Never***, spring 2024
- about courage and regret, danger and desire, about choosing

Available through Daniel Boone Footsteps
**www.danielboonefootsteps.com**
**www.RandellJones.com**
1959 N. Peace Haven Rd., #105
Winston-Salem, NC  27106

# Foolhardy

Randell Jones, editor

**Daniel Boone Footsteps**
Winston-Salem, North Carolina

Copyrights retained by each writer for own stories
Permissions granted to Daniel Boone Footsteps
for publishing in this anthology

Compilation Copyright 2024, Daniel Boone Footsteps
All Rights Reserved
ISBN: 979-8-9902784-2-4

Daniel Boone Footsteps
1959 N. Peace Haven Rd., #105
Winston-Salem, NC 27106

RandellJones.com
DanielBooneFootsteps.com
DBooneFootsteps@gmail.com

Cover image courtesy of *Shutterstock.com*

*The brave person,*
*if they be compared with the coward,*
*seems foolhardy;*
*and, if with the foolhardy person,*
*seems a coward.*
— *Aristotle*

# Preface

This book is the 11th in a series of anthologies, collections of personal stories on a set theme, our Personal Story Publishing Project. Since beginning in 2018, our collections have included these titles:

*Bearing Up,*  *Curious Stuff,*
*Exploring,*  *Twists and Turns,*
*That Southern Thing,*  *Lost & Found,*
*Luck and Opportunity,*  *Sooner or Later, and*
*Trouble,*  *Now or Never.*

This book comes from our 11th Call for Personal Stories, this one on the theme: "Foolhardy—personal stories of derring-do, desperation, and disaster—or not."

We thank the scores of writers who responded to the call by submitting such interesting, thoughtful, and well-crafted stories. They delivered the diversity and depth of perspective we were hoping for and the insight to self which proved we chose the right theme. Each story is about 750-800 words, so the writers were challenged in executing their craft, telling an interesting story succinctly. The writers and we have all found the Personal Story Publishing Project through its 11 iterations, so far, to be an instructive and rewarding writing experience. For the readers, it is a delight.

We received submissions from many writers in North Carolina and across the South, notably, but also from writers reaching across the country from Florida, Pennsylvania, and New York to the West Coast. We wish we could have printed them all, but we are delighted to curate 45 stories for this collection.

In June 2019, we launched a second outlet for sharing these fine writers with a broader audience. Their work can now be heard in our twice weekly podcast, "6-minute Stories." Our podcast is available through Apple Podcasts (iTunes), Spotify, and Stitcher. You can listen directly to "6-minute Stories" and find all the stories archived at RandellJones.com/6minutestories. Episodes are announced on Facebook @6minutestories.

*Now or Never*, the Personal Story Publishing Project, and "6-minute Stories" podcast are undertaken by author and publisher Randell Jones, doing business as Daniel Boone Footsteps in Winston-Salem, North Carolina.

Thank you for enjoying and appreciating good storytelling. And, remember…
    **Everybody loves a good story.**sm •

# Contents

Preface    vii
Contents    ix-xiv
Introduction    xv

A Fool in Love    1
    by Terri Kirby Erickson, Pfafftown, NC
    — *Is love worth the pain?*

When Things Got Crazy (*Dingue*)    5
    by David Collins, Pineville, NC
    — *Not what we expected*

The Bottle Rocket War    9
    by Richard L. Davis, Elk Grove, CA
    — *firecrackers on a stick, launched from tequila bottles!*

No Turning Back    13
    by Bruce Spang, Candler, NC
    — *What was I doing here? I'd been a fool to come.*

Time To Live or Die    17
    by Edward von Koenigseck, Ticonderoga, NY
    — *"Quick! Let's get the oars!"*

Outgunned    21
    by Jamie Cheshire, Winston-Salem, NC
    — *We had our audience!*

Mountain Panic     25
    by Suzanne Adams, Charlotte, NC
       – *I began to pass little crosses made of sticks and string.*

Greyhound to Ithaca     29
    by Maureen Ryan Griffin, Charlotte, NC
       – *I had a layover in Elmira, New York—six hours long.*

The Height of Foolishness     33
    by Mary Clements Fisher, Cupertino, CA
       – *I became daring in the dark.*

Listen Up!     37
    by Kenneth Chamlee, Mills River, NC
       – *"Don't panic. Keep your feet up."*

Fool's Hill     41
    by Caroline Kane Kenna, Huntersville, NC
       – *We were trying out young adulthood, but there were rules.*

My First Adventure     45
    by Akira Odani, St. Augustine, FL
       – *Should I tell my mother what I decided to do?*

Rum Punch and Reefers     49
    by Arlene Mandell, Linville, NC
       – *Oh, what the hell—go be one of the guys!*

When I Was a Yard Dog     53
    by David Lusk, Winston-Salem, NC
       – *I had a dream fueled by hope but mostly idealistic naïveté.*

Dismissed     57
     by Annette L. Brown, Atwater, CA
     — *Darlin', that's a championship team.*

Naked Relief     61
     by Jena Reger, Durham, NC
     — *I can't remember who suggested we go skinny dipping.*

Open Mouth, Insert Footlong Garden Hose     65
     by Nick Sipe, Gastonia, NC
     — *You durn fool*

Eavesdropping     69
     by Eloise Currie, Raleigh, NC
     — *I had to continue this risky addiction to their conversations.*

A Hundred Percent     73
     by Lisa Williams Kline, Davidson, NC
     — *Forty miles to spare*

No Stopping To Think     77
     by Thomas Gery, Reading, PA
     — *"I know what is coming."*

Williams Adventures     81
     by, Ginny Foard, Sullivan's Island, SC
     — *The siren song of the unknown called.*

Fallout     85
     by Suzanne Cottrell, Oxford, NC
     — *"All clear! Time for math."*

A Place To Hang Out                                89
    by Joe Brown, Bethania, NC
      – *"Did you get one?"*

You Think You Can Be a Housekeeper?        93
    by Evelyn Eickmeyer-Quiñones, Rock Hill, SC
      – *Why not? I thought.*

Gladys—Rolling Down the Highway           97
    by Jeanne VanBuren, Winston-Salem, NC
      – *I was now going somewhere; out of there, for sure.*

Risky Decisions                                        101
    by Susan W. Harris, Hilton Head Island, SC
      – *The car stopped; my heart pounded.*

God Winked                                            105
    by John Rumbold, Mooresville, NC
      – *I was taken aback, dumbstruck.*

How Bad Could It Be?                        109
    by Phyliss Grady Adcock, Morehead City, NC
      – *You can't imagine!*

Band of Brothers                                 113
    by Janice Luckey, Mooresville, NC
      – *Could they have once been scamps?*

The Empire of Death                           117
    by Erika Hoffman, Chapel Hill, NC
      – *"Mama, I don't want to die down here."*

Our Little Bit of Heaven 121
    by Janet K. Baxter, Kings Mountain, NC
        — *The location and land were doable. I barely looked at the house.*

Double Trouble 125
    by Barbara Houston, Matthews, NC
        — *What could possibly go wrong?*

They Say It's Like Riding a Bike 129
    by Frances Rinaldi, Mooresville, NC
        — *I was taking on challenges, all for my one secret event.*

Class V 133
    by Jane Satchell McAlister, Mocksville, NC
        — *Lives are lost on the river.*

Partners 137
    by Robin Russell Gaiser, Asheville, NC
        — *"Oh, I never leave home without it. There's danger out there."*

Up in the Air 141
    by S. G. Benson, Warne, NC
        — *It looked like a go-kart with wings and a parachute..*

The General 145
    by Peter Holsapple, Durham, NC
        — *He drove and hollered, and I cowered.*

On What Not To Do When Traveling 149
    by Mirinda Kossoff, Pittsboro, NC
        — *"Well, have you got any better ideas?"*

Roped In     153
    by Alison Rice Bruster, Fort Mill, SC
    — *"How long have you been rock climbing?"*

Professor Curmudgeon     157
    by Bob Amason, St. Augustine, FL
    — *"Don't mind him. He's just crotchety like that."*

Here's a Deep Hole     161
    by Jim Riggs, Hilton Head Island, SC
    — *As I hit the water, I glanced back over my shoulder.*

The Backward High     165
    by David Inserra, Hilton Head Island, SC
    — *He called me scaredy pants.*

Never Take a Snapping Turtle for a Ride     169
    by Sondra Edwards, Boone, NC
    — *"Do not let it get to the pond. It will eat our fish!"*

Accidental Degrees and Grandmother Time     173
    by Susie Wilde, Greensboro, NC
    — *"Do one, not both."*

Just One More Thing     177
    by Randell Jones, Winston-Salem, NC
    — *I could hardly hold my head up.*

# Introduction

Foolhardy – whether we are or not is a matter of perspective and often known only after the fact, after everything stops. It could be a daring risk-filled accomplishment in the face of calculated odds, or a lucky slipping through the gates of doom by the skin of our teeth. In all cases, we reap rewards or suffer the costs, getting the good and the bad, and settle the matter afterward by asking if it was worth it. The difference between hero and victim is yet to be determined, by us in the thick of it and by those watching from afar.

To some, foolhardy is a challenge, a beckoning to prove the world is wrong about us that we are brave enough, strong enough, smart enough, good enough to win despite the odds and to vanquish doubt, receive the spoils for our valor however that might be measured—in accolades, in prize money, or just the chance to live another day.

To others, foolhardy is imprudence unleashed, disregard for the rules and the guardrails that keep us from going over the edge, doing the unimaginably stupid and being proud of it, brandishing a false sense of invincibility as our weapon of choice in the fight for self-respect.

For still others, desperate, foolhardiness is not a choice, but something thrust upon them by circumstances. We find ourselves in a situation and know things have to change. In the words of Robert Frost, "The best way out is always through." And so we go, head down, full on, might against plight. Maybe we win, may we lose. We had to try; our backs were against the wall.

We are delighted by the response to our 11th Call for Personal Stories, and we are thankful to all the writers who invested time and energy into crafting personal stories for possible inclusion in this anthology. From among the submissions, we chose stories to include based on the quality of the writing and the resonance of the personal experiences shared with the announced theme, "Foolhardy—personal stories of derring-do, desperation, disaster—or not."

From the stories we have collected here, you will soon know something more about the label "foolhardy."

Foolhardy is taking a chance on love and sticking with it despite the inevitability of death. It's the foolishness of male youth on a spring day to put their manhood on display as part of the eternal mating ritual of the species. Foolhardy is the siren's song of world travel and the reassurance of embraceable time travel to reunite in spirit with long-gone generations of family.

Foolhardy is being egged on by siblings or peers and in a flash finding yourself running from an angry mob you just insulted, momentarily and likely being thrashed by a giant, spinning ship's propellor, or looking down with trembling trepidation after climbing a sky-high water tower by moonlight. It's jumping onto a raging torrent with no capacity for it to stop doing what it does best—kill you if you make one small mistake.

Foolhardy is doing battle face-to-face with the ideas your boss thinks are tried and true, the ones you regard as tired and rude. It's friendship in the face of imaginable dangers, while your friend—the one you have pledged to protect—has broken every agreed-upon rule. Foolhardy is leaving home with hope and grit and determination, knowing what you can do without to get what you most want—your own life on your own terms.

Foolhardy is believing that success comes to those who try and that along the way the universe gives you signs of reassurance. It is taking a chance on others to please yourself, trusting in the good nature of kindred souls, and watching the sunrise at a waterfall that was promised to be spectacular and was exactly that and more—it was memorable.

Foolhardy is thrashing around in the surf offshore, swimming in the altogether and leaving the security of your swimwear to chance on the beach. It is the unthinking act which spoils a long friendship for the rest of your life. Foolhardy is attempting to impose your human will upon another species whose instincts, strength, and determination you cannot imagine.

Foolhardy is a son's love for his mother, with enough courage to accept what is best for her in the face of real, heartfelt loss for himself. It is having the courage to acknowledge yourself and to be who you are despite whatever life you may have constructed before. Foolhardy is thinking quickly in every language you need to grease the palms of those who must be bribed so you can get back on the road.

Foolhardy is trying to solve a problem in a way that creates more trouble than you had before. It is making a success of a bad situation, making a haven out of troubled ground. It is a walk in somebody else's shoes and understanding why, of course, they have a pistol in their purse.

Foolhardy is embracing crochety and ill-tempered as desirable traits. It's running on fumes and having to rely on the kindness of strangers on a dark and lonely road. It's being a confident liar, or at least good enough to almost get away with it. It's mixing drugs and alcohol with work colleagues and sunny, tropical isles.

Foolhardy is a young grandson giving an uncertain answer to a short-tempered man. It's paying good money to descend deeper and deeper amidst the skulls and bones beneath the city streets. Foolhardy is tequila, bottle rockets, and 5-cent cigars spent in replaying key battles of the great world wars for education, of course, and also because the wives are away.

Foolhardy is many things and we each may be more of all that than we know. So, now it's your time to be such—brave enough to venture into experiencing vicariously the challenges faced by others and foolish enough to think that you might have done it differently. Either way, sometimes we are all a little foolhardy.

Enjoy. •

# A Fool in Love
## by Terri Kirby Erickson

I have never been known as a risk taker, even in childhood. If my parents told me not to do something, I usually didn't do it. There were a few early attempts to buck my propensity to avoid walking on the "wild side," including getting on a few scary rides at the fair, the worst of which was called, "The Octopus." Fortunately, my mother was a raving beauty—a cross between Candace Bergen and Ava Gardner, and when she saw her daughter whirling in circles, frozen in terror, my face turning a sickening shade of "puce," Mom (no doubt batting her eyelashes with considerable effect) convinced the operator to stop the ride. After that mortifying episode, I stuck to the merry-go-round and the chair lift.

In high school I never drank, smoked, or availed myself of the vast number of drugs available to young people in the '70s. I didn't go to parties, skip school, or date sketchy boys. I was in the National Honor Society, was a majorette, and my boyfriend was captain of the track team. I adored my family, had great friends, and thought everyone I loved most would live forever. The first people I cared about who died were my great-grandparents and my grandfathers, who both passed away at 57, which seemed old to me at the time. Even when my aunt died some years later at 44, a heartbreaking event for our family as well, I thought she was old, too. I was only 17 and 44 seemed like a million years away.

Then, in 1980, when I was 22, my 20-year-old brother who was my only sibling, was killed in a tragic accident. Three months later, my paternal grandmother, who was like a second mother to me, died of cancer. In my early 30s, my best friend since childhood was murdered by her estranged husband. As the years went by, I lost other good friends, along with my maternal grandmother, a cousin, two uncles, my in-laws, and the most painful of all my recent losses, my parents, Tom and Loretta Kirby, who died six months apart in 2019. I miss them so much.

Obviously, my belief in immortality for the people I adored did not pan out. I've lost my entire nuclear family now, and too many other people I love, of all ages, to count. So, while I still avoid risks to my personal safety and wellbeing (although I have had, since I was a child, an alphabetical list of health challenges, some of which should have killed me, too, but miraculously haven't yet) I go on loving people who are also not immortal, who I might lose any second for all sorts of reasons, including death, moving to Antarctica, or just drifting out of my life as friends will sometimes do.

So, it's not really true that I'm not a risk taker. Loving any mortal being is a bigger risk than bungee jumping, racecar driving, parachuting out of a plane, or swimming with sharks. People leave. People die. If you love someone and lose him or her, which you will do over and over again if you live long enough, you are going to suffer in ways you cannot imagine.

Grief is a weight you carry for a lifetime. You find ways to live with it, but it never ends. Of course, the time you spent with your loved ones was precious, the memories of them sweet. But when loss after loss knocks you to your knees, you have to ask yourself, is love worth the pain?

For me, the answer is a resounding yes. I would not trade one second with the people (or the pets) I've loved and lost. My brother was my dearest childhood companion. My wonderful parents were loving and supportive—there for me in every conceivable way, and I did my best to always be there for them. My grandparents taught me how to live and to age with strength, grace, and humor. And I spent so many nurturing, hilarious, and meaningful times with my late friends. As to the people I love who are still with us on this earth—my beloved husband of almost thirty-three years, our darling daughter and son-in-law, other family members and cherished friends, my life would be so empty, lonesome, and altogether less fun, without them.

So, while I will never run with the bulls, bet on horses or card games, ride another "Octopus," or even board a plane without anti-anxiety medication, feel free to call me a "foolhardy" risk taker—in love if nothing else. And if you are one of the people I love, you can be sure it will be without reservation, without hesitation, regardless of how long or short our time together, with all my foolish heart. •

Copyright 2024, Terri Kirby Erickson

Terri Kirby Erickson of Pfafftown, North Carolina, is the author of seven poetry collections, including her latest book, *Night Talks: New*

*A Fool in Love*

*& Selected Poems* (Press 53), a Finalist for the International Book Award for Poetry. Her work has appeared in "American Life in Poetry," *Atlanta Review*, *Rattle*, *The SUN*, *The Writer's Almanac*, *Valparaiso Poetry Review*, and numerous other publications. Winner of the Joy Harjo Poetry Prize, Nautilus Silver Book Award, and many others, her most recent awards are the *Annals of Internal Medicine* Poetry Prize and the Tennessee Williams Poetry Prize.

# When Things Got Crazy (*Dingue*)
## by David Collins

Coming of age in the 1960s, I spent a lot of time in darkened coffee houses, choking on the smoke, snapping my fingers to bad poetry, talking earnestly about imagery and symbolism in Antonioni and Fellini, Truffaut and Goddard—*auteurs* whose work I only half understood. At best. But even then I knew that for me those films were literally and metaphorically foreign, that I would never experience the kinds of things I was seeing on screen.

That changed in 1967 when my soon-to-be wife and I watched Audrey Hepburn and Albert Finney in *Two for the Road*. Too much in love to credit the darker parts of the storyline, we focused on the summer they met, hitchhiked together across France, fell in love and decided to marry.

That, we decided then and there, would be our honeymoon. Married in June 1968, we flew out of Boston and into the night. In the cargo hold, our too-heavy backpacks. In our pockets, too little money. Hell-bound for a summer of adventure in France, we didn't care.

That's when things got crazy.

Coming into France from Belgium, we found ourselves that first night at a *camping* near Dunkirk. "Don't walk on the beach," the man in charge warned as we checked in. When I asked why, he had a ready answer. "Mines. Left over from the war. People have been killed." In Rouen, our next stop, the one-eyed woman in charge of the small hotel where we tried to book a room took one look at my blond hair, concluded I was German, and turned us away. What Faulkner said about the past.

A kindly man who went out of his way to drive us to *le camping* in Amiens took us first on a tour of the city's poorer neighborhoods, tumbledown houses and communal wells that took the place of indoor plumbing, the perfect backdrop for his extended lecture on why we should embrace communism. When we camped by the side of the causeway at Mt. St. Michel, our open fire caught the attention of the locals. We were almost arrested.

*Not what we expected*, we thought as *le Métro* carried us into the center of Paris. *Paris will be less crazy*. It wasn't.

Busy with school and wedding preparations, we had paid too little attention to current events in France. We knew about *les Evénéments de mai*, about the students and workers who had joined forces to protest antiquated rules and regulations. We didn't know that when we emerged from the underground at the Place St. Michel the square would be swarming with uniforms, that the *Compagnies Républicaines de Sécurité*, riot police infamous for their brutality, had been brought in to keep the city kids in line.

Every night for a week we joined the French students marching in the streets, chanted anti-government slogans and joyfully defied authority. Until the tear gas flew. Until the CRS raised their batons and chased us through the streets, eyes and lungs burning from the gas.

*Not what we expected*, we thought as we stood by the side of the road, thumbs out, bound for the Côte d'Azur. Things will calm down in the south.

We rode in rickety *Deux-Chevaux* with French students high on politics and a variety of other things, sang the *Marseillaise* and the *Internationale* as the miles rolled by. We rode on winding roads with truckers convinced both lanes were theirs. We spent two days and more in a small town somewhere in *les montagnes noires* as car after car after car sped by raising the dust around us. My wife fended off propositions from aging Frenchmen whose leering eyes should have been warning enough.

It was in the south that things really got crazy.

We were standing, as ever, by the side of the road, thumbs out, when a convoy of trucks rolled by. French soldiers on a training exercise. As the last truck passed, we watched as a small ball tossed from the back bounced across the road toward us. We tracked the ball, bounce by bounce, closer and closer.

Until we realized that the thing bouncing toward us was a hand grenade.

I pushed my wife into the ditch by the side of the road, kicked the grenade as hard as I could and joined her. Seconds later, the grenade did what hand grenades do. It exploded. The bang rang in our ears. White powder flew everywhere. A practice grenade. Hard to tell the difference when you have only seconds to react.

It was all over in a flash. That moment with the hand grenade, that crazy summer in France. Only the memories remain. And the question people ask when, spurred on by too many glasses of wine, I tell the story: "Would you do it again?"

Edith Piaf gave me the answer in a song even older than my story. "*Je ne regrette rien*." •

Copyright 2024, David Collins

David Collins holds a Ph.D. in English from the University of Wisconsin–Madison and taught English/Creative Writing for forty years. His work has appeared in numerous journals, reviews, magazines, and newspapers. His first full-length book, *Accidental Activists: Mark Phariss, Vic Holmes, and Their Fight for Marriage Equality in Texas*, won the Mayborn Award for Excellence in Nonfiction in 2016, published in 2017 by the University of North Texas Press.

David is the immediate-past president of Charlotte Writers Club and makes his home in Pineville, North Carolina, with his wife, Jean, and their rambunctious Labrador retriever pup.

# The Bottle Rocket War
## by Richard L. Davis

"No plan survives first contact with the enemy," wrote Field Marshal Erwin Rommel in his *Infantry Attacks* (1937). He has a point, but it does not mean the unexpected—or the unconventional—cannot yield absolute victory!

The year was 1970, half a century ago, and friends David, Morgan, Dennis, and I had traveled to Playa Mona Lisa Beach, near Ensenada, Mexico, for a long weekend with our respective First Wives. We needed a break—the era then wallowed deep in a darkened realm of platform shoes, bellbottom pants, and Nehru jackets. Leisure suits had yet to reach their height, but miniskirts were deliciously in vogue, and each of our First Wives had a very nice pair of legs.

The first few days were fun with dining together, walking around town, glad conversation, and laughter. But when the First Wives decided to shop for ... anything—clothes, costume jewelry, black velvet paintings, whatever ... we four bored warriors took off on our own, seeking amusement and not a little mischief.

Several self-administered shots of tequila later (facilitated by a smiling 14-year-old bartender), we found ourselves before a local street vendor who sold bottle rockets—basically firecrackers on a stick, launched from … tequila bottles! Our martial enthusiasm thus inspired, each of us bought a fistful. However, we could find only one match among us to light all the rockets; so, one of us (probably me) came up with the idea of buying cigars to share. We splurged, buying the cheapest 5-cent cigars we could find.

Suitably armed and puffing now-lit cigars, we chose sides and squared off to build our competing castles among vacant sand dunes along the beach. David and Morgan paired as the obligatory opposition and trotted off to prepare their battlements. To defend honor, maidenhood, and the future of Western civilization, I joined Dennis, my Best Friend Forever. We, too, commenced to prepare for the expected onslaught.

With a cautious eye Dennis peered over the fragile threshold of our now invincible fortress. "I can see them both," he whispered. "They are not moving."

That was fine with me—we occupied the high ground and had clear visibility in all directions. Even better, Rommel's book said the situation meant our victory was assured! Maybe.

Our plan was to begin the engagement with a flurry of massive firepower. Then, while Dennis held the line, I would take Rommel's advice and use speed and secrecy to slip unnoticed to the left, flank the enemy out of position, and win the war! Simple.

Bottle rockets once launched went everywhere except where aimed. Hissing arcs of fire and smoke brightened further the sunlit sky. Some exploded in the air. Some did so as they smashed into the ground. None hit our opponents, nor did any of their return fire come anywhere close to us.

A rush of histrionic excitement followed. I imagined Dennis and me defending Fort McHenry during the War of 1812. David and Morgan embodied the nasty invading British, except they wore shorts and flip-flops and had no three-masted frigates. And we had no 8-foot masonry ramparts or grand battle-scarred garrison flag or Francis Scott Key to record our glory and legacy.

But we did have the proud red glare, blossoming through a profligate and noisy display of rockets!

In the excitement I puffed heavily on my cigar to help keep our initial barrage flying. As I ducked down for my planned flanking of the enemy, the sudden movement plus my cigar prompted a bilious nausea to form, characteristic of swallowing cigar smoke. This distraction prompted me to turn from the great battle and seek a hole in the sand suitable to receive an emerging visceral deposit.

Our opponents, however, did not accommodate groping for such a sandy solace under the hot Baja sun.

"Get back here," Dennis yelled. "They're coming! Fast!"

I looked at him but failed to find his argument compelling. I could feel my gills blossoming green.

David and Morgan shortly mounted our sandy parapets with a loud, eager shout. I did not care. A better part of my lunch, plus tainted tequila, proceeded to fill the beautiful hole in front of me. Seeing this, our attackers froze in their steps, then retreated in disgust, followed shortly thereafter by my now disgruntled Best Friend Forever. I was left alone in our well-defended ramparts, knowing we had won! … albeit a pleasure somewhat tempered by the pain in my gut.

So, "Mission Accomplished!" to quote a famous banner. *Thank you, Rommel!*

I next recall my First Wife appearing by my side with a wet cloth and a scowl on her face. I leave it to the reader to conjure what our First Wives collectively thought of all this.

Meanwhile, I'm still waiting for my medal. •

Copyright 2024, Richard L. Davis

Richard ("Rick") Davis is a retired Air Force colonel with an extensive professional writing history, including some non-fiction material published over the past 40 years. To transition to fiction, he studied with Amherst Writers & Artists and published his first novella in 2014. "The Bottle Rocket War" marks his third offering to PSPP, which earlier accepted his submissions for *Lost & Found* (spring 2023) and *Now or Never* (spring 2024). He lives in Elk Grove, California, with his Himalayan cat, Phoebe, and his aging collection of bottle rocket sticks.

# No Turning Back
## by Bruce Spang

I'd driven by the house several times. The lights on. Doorway lit. Cars in driveway. Figures moved back and forth in the bay window. One part of my mind kept saying, "Stop. Pull over." The other part told me, "This is too much. Go back home." I agreed. All I had to do was keep going to the end of the street, turn right, drive a few hundred yards, turn left, and be on 95 north.

But driving home was no answer. Half the furniture had been loaded onto a truck and brought to my wife's new home. I still called her my wife since we were, as yet, not divorced. My son and daughter lived with me part of the week and with her the other half. The day she moved her things out of the house I'd spent in Ogunquit on the beach barefoot. The cool November sand between my toes. Rocks tossed in the surf. I went to a bar, sat by a window, looking at the waves draw back the tide.

I arrived at the house thinking, I can cope. It's all a process. But when I went to the master bedroom, I halted. The bed stood there as it had for decades. The same comforter, same headboard, footboard, legs. I slammed my fist into the door jam.

I called a friend, told him I had to move the bed, had to get it out of the room or I was going to go mad.

"Take a breath," he said. "It's late. We can do it tomorrow."

"No. Now."

We took the bed apart, carried it downstairs, moved the couch out of the den into the dining room, shifted my son's bed into my old bedroom. It was like carrying the corpse of my marriage. If it were in another room, maybe I could revive it.

I didn't want to return to it. Too much of the past haunted the rooms. I turned around, pulled in a driveway, and parked.

I could hear the words of Richard, "Just go. How will you ever find out unless you do?" We'd met at the Hungry Dragon restaurant. I asked him if there was any group I could join. I didn't want to be scrounging around in a bar trying to find someone. I wanted to meet adults, ones who had their life together.

He patted my hand. "I have the perfect place."

Here I was, late for their meeting, outside on the sidewalk, the front door twenty feet away, hands in pockets, heart in my mouth, sweating. For forty-six years I had denied myself, or part of myself, or maybe the whole of myself. My denial ran deep into my past with a current so strong that to get by and away from it, felt as if I'd drown if I wasn't careful.

I knocked on the door. A man, tall with a pleasant smile, greeted me, shaking my hand. His fingers were long and soft, easy to grasp.

"Come in." He took my coat. "New here?"

"Yes."

He gave me his name—Marion. He pointed to a back room with a fireplace. There were fifteen people. Some in small groups. Some on the couch. Several on the floor.

"Let me introduce you," he said. "We're just getting started."

Not good with names—Nathan and Leo, Janet and Barbara, Nick and Sabastian—flashed into my head and out in rapid order. What struck me was that they were couples with children of their own. But they were not typical couples. They were gay. I was in a room filled with gay parents who met to discuss how to cope with the trials of raising children whose parents were stigmatized.

"Is something wrong?" Marion asked.

I was sweating. My body on overdrive. What was I doing here? I'd been a fool to come. I wanted to turn on my heels and get back in the car, back to my old life.

Marion pulled me aside, taking me to the kitchen. He looked at me intently. "This is all new to you, right? I remember well. I was petrified the first time I came to a meeting.

*No Turning Back*

Married twenty-years. I was still at war inside myself. Lonely. Scared. You name it. Sound familiar?"

I broke into tears. He opened his arms and I folded into them, no longer the only fool in the room. •

Copyright 2024, Bruce Spang

Bruce Spang, former Poet Laureate of Portland, Maine, is the author of two novels, *The Deception of the Thrush* and *Those Close Beside Me*. His most recent collection of poems, *All You'll Derive: A Caregiver's Journey*, was jpublished in 2024. He is the poetry and fiction editor of the *Smoky Blue Literary and Arts Magazine*. He teaches courses in fiction and poetry at Great Smokies Writing Program at University of North Carolina in Asheville and lives in Candler, NC with his husband Myles Rightmire and their five dogs, five fish, and thirty birds.

# Time To Live or Die
## by Edward von Koenigseck

Patience ... watching the channel, hoping to see one approaching. My 12-year-old brother Skinner and I, 10 years old, found this challenge the most daring thing we could ever do.

Sightings were erratic; we couldn't watch the channel every minute of every day. Small oil tankers navigating our shallow waters were our targets, easy to spot from a distance. The channel ran a mile west before it passed from view. It ran the same distance east to where tankers docked at Oil City, the local oil depot storage area. Our location let us get our rowboat out and ready near the channel's center as passing tankers headed toward Oil City or the Atlantic Ocean.

We had performed this daring act numerous times. Each trip offered challenge; timing was everything. Skinner, the strongest, manned the oars to catch large eddies swirling behind the tanker's stern as it passed. Eastbound oil-laden tankers were deeply immersed in the channel waters. Westbound empty tankers rode higher out of the water and were faster, creating larger cresting waves and eddies.

We frequently played in the empty lot across the street from our house. Its north side had a decrepit retaining wall. Some vertical posts remained standing at the water's edge where we moored our rowboat. One day, looking toward the east Skinner's attention fixated on something. He pointed toward Oil City and shouted, "Ed! A tanker!" and began running toward our house shouting, "Quick! Let's get the oars!"

We raced home, grabbed the oars and ran to our docked 14-foot rowboat. Skinner jumped in first and I handed him the oars. Untying bow and stern ropes from home-made outriggers, we shoved away from the shoreline. Skinner sat on the rower's seat, facing me and I sat on the stern-mounted seat facing forward.

Skinner put his back into rowing, feet braced along the boat's side ribs for support. Rowing hard in the calm waters, we approached the channel's center. With eyes on the approaching tanker, we were in position before the tanker arrived so its starboard side would be broadside to us. Traveling fast, the tanker's bow tossed large white-capped waves. Skinner would keep the rowboat about fifty feet from the passing tanker's starboard side. Timing became critical once the center of the starboard side was even with us. At that point, Skinner rowed directly to where the starboard side of the tanker's stern would be. He intended to get sufficiently close to the large, partially exposed propeller blades, for us to ride the huge swirling eddies, with us avoiding what we thought might be a great propeller undertow. The whirling, vicious-looking blades stuck out of the water about five feet. When the tanker passed, we hoped to be even with the stern's center by which time it was ahead at least fifty to sixty feet and racing away. Once in the middle of the eddies, Skinner would stop rowing and our small boat would be spun like a top by the still powerful eddies for several revolutions.

On previous adventures I had never seriously worried about getting too close to the propellers even though some of the tanker's crews had yelled at us. What I didn't know was this time Skinner decided to do everything he could to get as close to the props as possible. In a fury he strained at the oars, ignoring the tanker's large cresting waves while our rowboat bounced as it cut through the crests and troths. About 15 feet from the stern we heard crewmen leaning over the tanker's stern, yelling and waving their arms for us to get away.
The ship's loud horn tooted as a warning, but Skinner ignored everything. The tanker's stern passed us by about 10 feet. Finally realizing what Skinner was doing, I screamed at him in terror to drop back. The rotating propeller blades made loud swishing noises as they thrashed the water, frightening me so badly I thought I might pee in my pants. Ignoring my plea, Skinner continued toward the center of the eddies while I contemplated death by heart attack or chopping blades.

Some of the crew still leaning over the stern continued shouting, waving fists in the air and cursing us as the tanker pulled away. Once in the center of the eddies, Skinner stopped rowing, and still holding the oars, stood up, raised his arms, and screamed, "We did it!" as the eddies rapidly spun us around. Realizing we were not going to die, I tried to enjoy the circus-like rotation which lasted about a minute.

While rowing homeward Skinner admitted, "You know, Ed, for a moment I was really scared we were too close to the propellers and might get dragged under and chopped up." •

Copyright 2024, Edward von Koenigseck

Edward von Koenigseck, relocated from Florida, resides in Ticonderoga, New York. Having a 40-year career in technical publications, he also published two books *(Technical Writing for Private Industry* and *Island Park, a Memoir,* and four short stories. He created 92 one-hour lectures on biblical history for presentation to elders, sponsored by the non-profit Florida-based Shepherd Centers organization. He also created and taught two semesters on technical writing for advanced English students at Florida Institute of Technology, is an editor, and is currently writing a novel, a biography, and an autobiography.

# Outgunned

by Jamie Cheshire

We didn't know we were outgunned.

If we'd been sold out, it was probably that guy who was always running his mouth and bragging. I wouldn't say there's a jerk in every crowd, but when an entire floor of college boys is gathered up, naked, in a dormitory stairwell ready to run the hall of the girls' floor below them—and one of them has a red ribbon tied around his willy—if one's a jerk it's probably him.

With big, wide windows and shiny terrazzo floors, ECU's Umstead dorm kept the old school appeal the newer dorms lacked. In 1975, we learned girls would be living on the second floor. We called it coed and thought it meant opportunity. But it hardly turned out to be what we thought.

Even so, life in Umstead was idyllic. We had little responsibility. The dining halls made the food, laundry service was available, facilities crews did the rest, and we took it all for granted just like we did our families.

We'd all lived easily together for months when spring floated into Greenville on the breezes of '76. I'm not sure if we were

going on a dominance run or thought we would accomplish
something, or what. But we were nutted up and decided
to streak the girls. We had no end game. We were going
to streak the girls and then go back upstairs and get stoned.

That's not what happened.

They might've been tipped off, but I doubt it. I mean, Ribbons
might have talked. He had to borrow it from somewhere.
Guys didn't keep ribbon. And this wasn't a little nest of curling
ribbon he had. No, this was a big, wide, shiny red ribbon,
way too big for the package.

But nobody told. We were seen in the stairs and realized
it was now or never. We'd been shuffling together, looking
for courage for several minutes—filling the stairwell in uneasy
proximity. It would've been weird to just turn around and walk
back to our rooms together naked.

Everything went according to plan until the last guys rounded
the corner. I guess. I didn't look back. What I saw was all the
doors standing open and all the young women lined up in them
like a parade had been announced. We had our audience!
What could be more disappointing than running naked past
a lot of closed doors?

Well… uh-oh!

In every doorway, the women waiting for us were holding
empty pitchers. Bold and triumphant, we didn't see those
gleaming terrazzo floors were gleaming wet and our naked,

headlong herd lost its footing all at once and fell into big, ugly piles sliding down the hallway under the curtain of their laughter.

Dominance abandoned us for the girls' team.

What do you do when your mission is compromised?
You have an exit strategy, right?

There were stairways on each end and one in the middle, so no problem. The way out is to keep going.

I still don't know how those young women had time to fill all those pitchers, flood all those floors and wire all those stairway doors shut. But whatever they did in a few seconds, time stopped for us. Somebody finally fought one of the doors open and most of the guys ran home, ribs bruised and tails tucked.

But some of us had been captured. We could not run home naked. No, we were caught and pressed into exhausting service behind doors which now swiftly closed. Only much later were we allowed out to make our way back upstairs, wearing borrowed towels or sissy, ill-fitting robes.

That was decades ago. Many of the women I know now have become grandmothers. I knew some of this generation's grandmothers uniquely well when they were 19. I lived one floor above them.

We think of grandmothers as ageless and timeless. We're sure they've always been wise, cotton soft, never wild, and fragrant of powder and salve. We cherish an image of grandmothers as mild, sinless, patiently indulgent, perfect in love, fierce when necessary and sometimes maybe just a little bit witchy.

But look deeper. There's a lifetime in those eyes.

If you think she was always old and could always be found watering the potted lantana on her sunny porch or friending the cats in her back garden, or if you think she has always been waiting for you in a halo of awning light on her back stoop—ok, yes, she has---but if you think it without considering that before she chose this, there were other gardens and other cats, other porches and other lights, and that the screen door likely slammed shut behind her more than once when she left, you might should think again.

Her story is probably not exactly this. But she remembers.

And you're still outgunned. •


Copyright 2024, Jamie Cheshire

Fascinated with every big and little thing, Jamie Cheshire has long been an avid student of design and structure. Having worked together with giants, he has had the extreme good fortune to practice his craft for most of the last four decades and has seen his work appear nationally and in several countries on three continents. He lives in Winston-Salem, North Carolina, with his beloved feral, hippie-chick wife, their three dogs and two cats. Deeply committed to the ordinary, he is constantly searching for a way to describe it.

Editor's note: ECU is East Carolina University in Greenville, NC.

FOOLHARDY

# Mountain Panic
## by Suzanne Adams

The *Lötschental* is haunted. The rest of Switzerland is cheery, all cuckoo clocks and chocolate, but the *Lötschental* is dark, a spooky valley between oppressive mountain peaks. Walking sticks are ubiquitous in Switzerland, but the ones from the *Lötschental* are twisted and carved with tortured, devilish faces. The whole place feels eerie. Who would want to go there? Me.

Above the *Lötschental* is a trail system that ascends the high country and stretches from one mountain hut, or *bergerhütli*, across the glaciers to the next one. The *bergerhütlis* are maintained by Swiss hiking clubs and are open to anyone. What an adventure, to start in the *Lötschental*, climb the trail, sleep in a *bergerhütli* and trek across frozen glaciers to the next hut, by myself! I was free from studies for a week and was eager to learn something not in books.

I took the train from Zurich with my new backpack, sleeping bag, food for a week, and warm clothes. My train car was empty except for a drunken woman who hung onto a strap and kept proclaiming, "I AM AUSTRIA!" Okay, then — *I was AMERICA*. Invulnerable.

The train reached the *Lötschental* in the early afternoon. I had plenty of time to reach the *bergerhütli* before it became seriously dark. And the *bergerhütlis*, unlike the inns in town, are free. So, I started up the trail.

At first it felt really good—the air was crisp but not too cold, the snow underfoot was packed but not slippery. It was 1975 and I felt young and strong.

The path curved up and away from the small town below. I began to pass little crosses made of sticks and string, crafted by shepherds who spend months in the mountains alone with their flocks. I'd read that in their lonely lives shepherds occasionally experienced extreme terror for no apparent reason. In the grip of this "mountain panic" they would sometimes act irrationally. The local custom was to make crosses for protection and comfort. I smiled at the crosses as I passed.

It was beginning to snow, lightly at first, nothing serious. The twilight would last for another hour at least. Plenty of time to reach the hut safely. My footprints began to disappear behind me, as the snow fell more heavily. Up and up the winding path with switchbacks threaded its way along the mountainside, the increasingly steep descents only partially obscured by low bushes. It was getting dark, but the path was still visible, and I was in no real danger.

I reached the mountain hut; it was unlocked as promised. Inside that sturdily constructed wooden shelter were blankets, firewood and emergency rations. It was astonishingly quiet.

I could almost taste the quiet. All I needed to do was put some logs in the fireplace and light them, warm up my dinner, unroll my sleeping bag and nestle in. This was the adventure I had planned, and here I was, having it.

I signed the guest log and noticed no visitors had been there for months. It was fully dark outside now, a blackness unrelieved by any shaft of human-created light. I could feel my heart beating harder. The very walls of the hut, those protecting me from the snowstorm, seemed threatening.

But there was no real threat. The only possible danger would be if I tried to go back down the mountain in the dark, in the snow, where fresh drifts obscured the path.

And yet I found myself putting my boots back on, packing my things and going to the door. I was aware that this was absolute idiocy. Nothing was wrong with my original plan. Crossing the glaciers at that time of year wouldn't have been hazardous. But going down the mountain alone at night in a snowstorm, that was dangerous. Stupid. It would be easy to stumble off the path and fall down a ravine. Or a cliff. And no one in the world would know where I was.

Nevertheless, I closed the shelter door behind me. Some weird force seemed to be pushing me. I had to get out of there, away from—what? But I had no choice. At first, I tried to force myself to walk slowly, using my walking stick to test the ground to make sure I was on the path. But I was beyond reason. I broke two branches from a pine tree and held them in a cross as I plummeted down the path, stumbling, wiping

*Mountain Panic*

snow from my eyes and straining to see.

Four hours later, I was down. I pounded on the door of an inn and got a place to stay for the night, never mind the cost.

I had wanted to learn something on this trip.

I did.

I am not invulnerable after all. •

Copyright 2024, Suzanne Adams

Suzanne Adams has been an actor, director, teacher, and archenemy of Mountain Pine Beetles in the Rockies. She didn't take writing semi-seriously until moving to Charlotte, in this "writingest state." Her stories have won a few prizes in literary contests and have been published in *Litmosphere*, *Main Street Rag*, *Memoirs Ink*, and *Minerva Rising*. She is an enthusiastic member of Charlotte Writers Club, Charlotte Lit, and North Carolina Writers Network, and is delighted to be included in this anthology.

# Greyhound to Ithaca
## by Maureen Ryan Griffin

One August afternoon in 1975, I boarded a Greyhound bus, headed to Cornell University to visit a high school friend. I'd enthusiastically accepted Dennis's invitation, but I was floundering, had struggled with depression throughout most of my first year of college. I'd gained at least 20 pounds and lost any self-confidence I'd ever had.

Shortly before dark, the bus rattled down yet another small main street, brakes squealing to a stop as they had been, town after town. This time, though, the driver said, "End of the line." When I looked at him, confused, he said, "Let me see your ticket" and then, "You have to transfer after your layover. Just wait out front. Your bus will have a sign for Elmira."

I checked my ticket. I had a layover in Elmira, New York, too—six hours long. How had I not wondered why the bus from Erie, Pennsylvania, didn't get to Ithaca until the next morning, even though Dennis mentioned it was a four-hour drive? Oh well. I would wait in the bus station.

But when we pulled in near midnight, it was closed. Panicked, I asked a fellow passenger what to do. "There's a Dunkin'

Donuts about ten blocks away," she said, pointing. "Take a left at the Shell Station and you'll see it." I started walking.

I'd worked at a Dunkin' Donuts in high school. The familiarity felt almost like a hug. I ordered coffee, pulled out *The Two Towers* and disappeared into Tolkien's wooded land of hobbits and elves, bravery and second breakfasts.

At some point, I looked up. Two long-haired, kind-eyed guys were looking at me.

"We've been wondering what you're reading," one of them said. "It must be good."

"It is! The second book of J.R.R. Tolkien's *The Lord of the Rings*."

They hadn't heard of it and listened attentively to my description. We talked about books, music, places we'd been. They loved the outdoors, too. When I said I was going to Ithaca, they told me about a beautiful waterfall there.

Before I knew it, it was 5:30. I put my book away, left my tip.

"We should drive you to the bus station," one of them said. "This isn't the best part of town."

It's been so many years, I don't remember their names. One was Joe, I'm fairly sure. The other, maybe Dave? And did I give a second thought to getting into their pickup?

When we got there, Joe or Maybe Dave said, "We're going to wait with you till your bus comes." We sat in the truck and kept on talking. When had I experienced such easy conversation?

A few minutes before my bus was scheduled to pull in, Maybe Dave or Joe said, "Hey, why don't we drive Maureen to Ithaca? It's not even an hour away. We can take her to the waterfall."

They assured me I'd get to the station before Dennis was expecting me. The bus would make numerous stops.

The sky blushed purple, then pink, then coral-gold, as we sped down the highway on our way to Ithaca. Just as the sun came up, the radio played John Denver's "Thank God I'm a Country Boy."

"I never liked this song," Maybe Dave or Joe said, "but right now it feels just right."

It did. I'd never felt happier, or safer, than I did with those two guys who did not seem to think that I was anything but beautiful just as I was. I can still hear the rousing response, "Yes! Let's take Maureen to Ithaca!" and still feel that safe. That happy.

The spray from the waterfall sparkled in the morning sun. Warblers, whistlers, and trillers sang. Joe and Maybe Dave knew when not to talk, too, when beauty itself was the conversation. I hugged them both when they dropped me off at the bus station in plenty of time.

*Greyhound to Ithaca*

Dennis was already there, dressed in belted chinos and a collared shirt, in stark contrast to my gauzy tunic top and baggy jeans. He wasn't happy to hear my story when he asked how I'd arrived before my bus. What kind of explanation was *I trusted my intuition*?

Dennis wasn't happy with anything about me. Not my decisions, not my ideas, not my weight, which he was not kind enough not to mention. It was a painful weekend. Our one conversation afterward, at our 25th high school reunion, was brief.

I never saw Joe or Maybe Dave again, but I do know to whom I'm grateful.

Yes, it could have been otherwise. I'm grateful as well for grace and good-heartedness and whatever else there is to praise that my trip to Ithaca still shimmers in my memory as a time of sheer joy, thanks to two long-haired, kind-eyed guys in t-shirts. Or . . . could they have been hobbits in disguise, on a quest to rescue someone from her tower of loneliness? •

Copyright 2024, Maureen Ryan Griffin

Maureen Ryan Griffin has loved words and stories since her "Cat in the Hat" days and leads writing workshops and retreats (www.WordPlayNow.com). She's published in numerous literary journals and, most recently, in 2024's *Chicken Soup for the Soul: Miracles, Angels and Messages from Heaven*. Her books include *Ten Thousand Cicadas Can't Be Wrong* (poetry); *Spinning Words into Gold* (writing guide); *How Do I Say Goodbye: A Companion in Grieving, Healing, and Gratitude*, and a daily journal practice, *TAG, I'M IT!* She and her husband, Richard, live in Charlotte, North Carolina.

# The Height of Foolishness
## by Mary Clements Fisher

I became daring in the dark. Gazing at the crisscross ladder to the town's water tank, I bowed my head and choked, "God help me." In the daylight, I played the perfect preacher's daughter. On Sundays, elder parishioners assessed my skirt a sensible length and my hair neither too short nor too long. My high school teachers praised my good grades; my parents expected nothing less. I scoffed at the six-pack sippers parked on deserted dirt roads. My drunken uncle's ruined life squashed any desire for drinking. Friends and frenemies alike teased me with "What a goody-two-shoes." Being good led to boredom, however. Boredom led to lowered defenses. Lowered defenses led to saying yes to this crazy dare in the dark.

One bold senior cheerleader, believing me braver than I was, swatted me on the bottom and handed me a magic marker to put my name next to hers. "Hey, kid. You've got this." Not one to disappoint, I tucked the marker in my bra.

"Yeah, I do." My churning stomach declared I didn't. Four steel trestles held the million-gallon tank and would handle one hundred pounds more. My trembling knees might not.

Swiping my sweaty hands on my shorts, I stared at my feet

and cursed. "Stupid strappy sandals," perfect for a summer Saturday night date but dead wrong for scaling a water tower. I slipped them off.

Four cheerleader girlfriends who'd dared me and three boys who'd stopped cruising the loop to see what was up, whooped and hollered. "Go, girl, go."

The south end of Main Street lay deserted except for these rowdies and me under a full moon. At midnight, children dreamed of flying or daring impossible heights without fear. With windows open on a sweltering August night, would their moms and dads stir with my friends' harangue, wake to my pounding heart, and call the sheriff or worse—my dad?

I stepped on the first metal bar and winced. The ragged edge cut into my arch. "Would anyone loan me their tennies?"

One of my buddies threw me her shoes. My stunt counted as primo weekend entertainment. Nobody wanted this party to end, except me.

Shoes tied, I dried my hands again on the back of my shorts and set one foot on the first rung and placed one hand over the other. Five feet off the ground and 160 to go. Doubts dried my mouth. Like being stuck in a broken, packed elevator, I suffered limited options, no wiggle room, and numbing panic. But no one ever could call me a quitter.

Halfway up, one of the boys whistled. I glanced down. Dizzy, I flattened my body and pressed my forehead against the cool girders. My grip froze. I gulped the moist night air and licked my lips. The crowd below grew quiet, like the moment a tightrope walker steps onto the rope without a net, wobbles, and hesitates.

I tilted my head to stare at the moon. Clouds slipped across its mocking face. No rocketing through space in my future, but damn it, I'd reach the top and return to earth again.

A breeze rustled the leaves of trees beneath me. My muscle memory kicked in. I clutched the next bar and the next, faster, and faster until I touched the railing circling the tank. Wrapping my left arm around the rail, I pulled out the marker, bit the top off, and spit it out. I scribbled my initials next to others on the tank and tossed the marker to my friends. They cheered. Not a permanent mark on the world stage but worth a bow. Letting go with one hand, I waved to my admirers and gasped.

Sweat trickled between my breasts. My soaked tee stuck to my back. An owl hooted. "Fool. Fool." If only I had wings. If only I'd said, "No way." If onlys and what ifs tortured me. What if my friends called for help? The gossip and shame if I stayed a prisoner on the tower until the fire department rescued me scared me more than falling. I faced my only option. Descend.

Crickets' chirping quieted my nerves. My mantra "Focus on your hands and feel with your feet" rolled off my tongue. Slow. Steady. My friends' murmurs drifted up and pulled me like gentle gravity. Down again until my toes touched the

*The Height of Foolishness*

ground. Brushing away hair plastered to my brow, I exhaled. "Haaaaa."

My girlfriends huddled around me, hugged me, and giggled, "Way to go, girl. You did it." Leaning against the car, the boys surveyed me with expressions akin to respect. I celebrated my mission accomplished with an audible "Alleluia." With an internal *never again*, I snuck home. In bed, I contemplated my miscalculation: No secrets survive in a small town. •

Copyright 2024, Mary Clements Fisher

Mary Clements Fisher celebrates her current mother/grandmother, sweetheart, student, and writer status in Cupertino, California. Two writers' groups Taste Life Twice and Daughters through the Decades support her mad, muddled, and magical moments of writing. She's published in *Quail Belle Magazine*, *Adanna Journal*, *Passager Journal*, *The Weekly Avocet*, *Prometheus Dreaming Journal*, *The Closed Eye Open*, *Capsule Stories*, *They Call Us Magazine*, and gratefully in several Personal Story Publishing Project books. Join her @maryfisherwrites and https://maryfisherwrites.squarespace.com/

# Listen Up
## by Kenneth Chamlee

After heavy overnight rain, the Gauley River in West Virginia was running fast and high, so our whitewater rafting trip promised an exhilarating day. My son and I geared up at the outfitter's check-in station: helmets, snug life jackets and closed-toe shoes, no flip-flops. The put-in spot was a 20-minute ride away in an old school bus.

While we bounced down a washed-out road, an old man in a tie-dye headband gave the safety lecture. He received the same astute attention that a flight attendant gets during a seat belt demonstration. Families were talking loudly and laughing nervously, but the graying river-runner did not demand attention. He kept talking at the same volume, and those who were close enough to hear, heard.

"Follow directions. Listen to your raft guide," he said ironically. "Keep a good grip on your paddle, but if you fall overboard, let it go. It will float and the guide will pick it up. Keep your feet pointed downstream. Don't try to stand or you might get a foot stuck in the rocks. The current will then push you under." It was becoming clear why we had signed three pages of waivers when we paid.

"If you find yourself under the raft when you fall out," the instructor continued, "don't panic. Keep your feet up and pull yourself backward to the rear of the raft." He made a hand-over-hand motion above his head, palms flat toward the bus's roof. "When you surface, the guide will pull you in."

The bus hit a few more jolting bumps, stopped with a lurch, and we were at the river. The Gauley was loud, churning, throwing up big waves, knocking back on itself. Our river guide, a fit young man named Devon, explained this was a working trip. We would be paddling hard, not just holding on. "Jam your sneaker between the bottom of the raft and the sidewall," he said. "Your hands will be busy, so this will help keep you in the raft." I looked at my son, his eyes wide and face grinning hugely.

A whitewater trip on a river that's "up and running" is a true thrill ride. It bucks and dips, pitches and plunges while cold water slams you every few seconds. Think of it as a continuous roller coaster with a firehose in your face and endless whoops of excitement. For an hour we rode the swirling peaks and troughs, responding vigorously when our guide yelled "Paddle left! Paddle right!" or the frequent "Everybody *dig!*"

Hitting one especially gnarly set of rapids, the raft jerked sharply, and my foot popped out of the secure spot it was wedged. I can't recall the somersault I must have made leaving the raft, but one second I was paddling and the next I was under water. For a moment I was disoriented because I thought I would just pop back up, but it was complete darkness. I was under the raft, moving with it just like the old guide had said.

The force of rushing water flattened me against the bottom of the raft. It was hard, rough rubber, like tire treads. Then I remembered—"Walk your hands toward the rear of the raft." I spread my palms against the coarse surface and pulled myself backwards. Working against the current was not easy. *This is taking too long!* I thought.

After three or four drawn-out "steps," I burst into daylight and gasped for air. Two strong arms grabbed the shoulders of my life jacket and flopped me aboard like a big grouper.

"Whoa!' Devon said. "You all right?"

"I think so, yes," I managed. "Thank you." I was shaking water out of my ears and checking my glasses when I saw my son's face. Its color matched the white of his helmet.

"Don't ever do that again," he said. "Ever." It was a flat, cold tone, an absolute directive.

"Unplanned stunt," I sputtered. "Not showing off." I started to grasp what had just happened, what could have happened, and what must have gone through his mind, if only for a few seconds.

The old river runner's safety speech probably saved my life. I remembered what he said at the precise moment I needed to.

*Listen Up*

Who knows what my reaction might have been in that sudden and desperate situation, without his bit of knowledge?

It is not foolhardy to go whitewater rafting with well-equipped, well-trained adventurers. But not listening to the cautions offered by their experience is. Sometimes being foolhardy is not the reckless action one takes, but the inaction, the deliberate dismissal, thinking "I got this," when one has no idea what "this" might prove to be. •

Copyright 2024, Kenneth Chamlee

A retired English professor, Kenneth Chamlee still enjoys teaching workshops on humor in poetry, writing in personae, and the remarkable connections between poetry and painting and photography. His poetic biography of 19th-century American landscape painter Albert Bierstadt, *The Best Material for the Artist in the World* (Stephen F. Austin State University Press, 2023), won the Outstanding Poetry Book Award from the National Cowboy and Western Heritage Museum. Ken is the author of *If Not These Things* (Kelsay Books, 2022), and his stories have appeared in several PSPP anthologies. Learn more at www.kennethchamlee.com.

# Fool's Hill
## by Caroline Kane Kenna

I don't think Andie ever told her mom about Marshall Tucker. God knows Mama never knew and if I'm honest, I wonder if telling it now is still breaking faith.

*Going fool's hill*, Andie's mom's expression for college escapades, she said it often, shaking her head. "Everyone goes up, it's how you come down, that matters." Mama's reply was simply, "live and learn." Mother lines for a girls' night out story, each of us would probably tell differently. My recollections of it come in flashes—mirror ball, an East Tennessee disco not too far from Bristol. Cherry and Andie, not the real names of my friends, but truth that ends after dawn with us safe in the dorm.

Those were the foolish, hill-climbing, let's-disco-down years of the late '70s, when we were trying out young adulthood, but there were rules. We go together, dance freely with whoever was there, and we leave together. Perhaps we agreed afterward never to speak of that full-moon ride again, Tucker's car hugging the backroads to his place. Cherry up front, Andie and I squeezed in the back because we were not letting our friend go alone, although she was determined to leave the disco with Marshall.

He's Marshall Tucker, the guy who sings "Devil Went Down to Georgia," Cherry told us in the disco ladies' room. After their first dance, Marshall Tucker had put his hat on our table and ordered a round of drinks, a clear violation of a no-guys-from-the-dance-floor-at-our-table rule. Her brown eyes were shiny with infatuation and alcohol. But Cherry's eyes were always shinier when a male was at the table—any table. Clever English major, funny when it was just girls, but add a guy, anyone's guy, to our mix and she dialed up charm and homed in on him.

Marshall was older than the usual college type she could beguile with the shift of a shoulder, a slow blink while listening to him talk. Perhaps he was a challenge for her, but you would think he would be immune to or at least wise to tactics Cherry seemed to be making up as she went along. Especially, if he was Marshall Tucker of band fame as he claimed.

Was the little voice screaming itself hoarse that night? If so, neither Andie or I heard it above the din of Donna Summer or knew enough to call Marshall's line what was. And then there was Cherry and this moon-eyed scheme. No talking her out of that, but we stick together. That was the deal.

Not one of us knew who the hell Tucker was or how this encounter could have been. A few weeks later, going somewhere in Cherry's car, the devil-fiddling song played, and a deejay intoned, *that was Charlie Daniels Band.* I clearly remember our conversation stopped, perhaps each of us revisiting that night, grateful we weren't headlines in the Bristol paper or a grid search for missing co-eds.

I see stupid tattooed on our foreheads; if I had told Mama, she might have said that before she hugged me hard. Guardian angels must have raced to make sure it turned out okay for Andie and me and Cherry too. After they slipped off, Andie and I clung to both ends of Marshall's couch and counted the miles back to the parking lot. Did she and I whisper about what ifs, and consider escapes that could have ended in unmarked graves? Maybe in our heads, but what I recall is moonlight through a picture window until we heard his door open, Marshall's deep, slow Tennessee twang, Andie and I waiting outside while he gathered keys. I remember his hat on Cherry's brown curls, the lonely road back, lane winding past a pond—gravel to highway and finally to Cherry's car. Marshall pulled up. He even got out and opened Cherry's door. Then he adjusted his belt, slapped Cherry's rump. She giggled, handed off his hat before he folded himself into his cockpit car and sped off.

Although Marshall let us believe the band lie, perhaps he wasn't such a bad sort. Or maybe our loyalty to Cherry tipped the scale? There was no conversation on our drive back. No mention of him, our lunacy, back at the dorm. It wasn't the last fool's hill for three of us that year, but it was an easy slide to the end of disco for me.

Mother lines I once rolled my eyes at, I doled out regularly to three sons as they made their own foolish ascents—"make good choices," my parting advice to each as they began their own trek. Knowing tumbles were likely. Hoping the way down wouldn't hurt too much and each would land safely—with stories they'll never tell me. •

*Fool's Hill*

Copyright 2024, Caroline Kane Kenna

Caroline Kane Kenna lives in Huntersville, North Carolina. A newspaper reporter before the internet. Stay-at-home Mom to three boys, trailing spouse for a corporate husband. Her family moved to Huntersville in 2005. Her writing has placed in Charlotte Writers Club contests. Poems published in *Above the Fold* and various *Kakalak* anthologies. Essays in *Reflections on the New River* and *The Love of Baseball* (McFarland 2015 & 2017.) A former president of Charlotte Writers Club, when she's not writing, she, her husband, and dog Guinness are RVing, or babysitting their first granddaughter.

# My First Adventure
## by Akira Odani

I came into this world as the second child, even though my older sister died a few months before my birth. My mother treasured me, I assume in hindsight, as the consolation for the lost baby. Every little movement of my infantile activities attracted my mother's attention. *Are you sick? Did you eat enough?* My eyes and ears, in turn, obsessed with her commands of dos and don'ts.

Her surveillance dissipated as soon as my two brothers arrived, one after another. When I was 5, I felt ignored. My mother appeared preoccupied with taking care of my siblings. To make it worse, one early afternoon, my mother ordered me a chore I detested—scooping up bullfrog eggs from the bottom of our lily pond. The ugly brown creatures, dozens, emitting low cow-mooing calls during the night, laid their translucent noodles of slimy and disgusting eggs. When dried on the ground under the sun, they stank like dead fish, blackish-green flies swarming around them.

Before I could protest, my mother handed me a fishing net with a long stick and disappeared into the kitchen. With little spirit, I dipped my fish net into the square pond. Then, an idea of a fun adventure popped into my head. *Why not visit my cousin?*

I recalled the fun-filled afternoon a few weeks ago running around the yard with her, Tadako, a girl one year older. She was the oldest of three children in her family, like I was in my family. We had the kinship of the oldest. She and her family visited us during the summer. Our two families saw each other on special occasions like memorial services for the deceased, Buddhist rituals, and New Year celebrations.

Although Tadako lived two hours away, I more or less knew how to get to her house by changing the local train to a trunk line. *Should I tell my mother what I decided to do? Would she worry about me?* I thought not.

I tossed the fishnet on top of the yucky goo, *bye-bye*, slithered out of the gate, and marched past the schoolyard to the commuter train depot. My little adventure gave my legs an encouraging bounce. A 5-year-old, less than one meter tall, I slipped through the turnstile without being noticed.

The train was relatively empty in mid-afternoon and had ample seats. I climbed onto a soft, long bench with my folded knees, turned around, and looked out the window. The fast-moving scenery of suburban neighborhoods, floating houses with their laundry in the yards, and green hedges exhilarated me. The rhythmic sound of wheels sliding on iron rails, *clickety-clack*, gave me the sensation of flying like a hawk. The conductor's low and confident voice, calling the next stop, assured me of the correct direction I was traveling. Other passengers appeared to consider me as one of them.

I reminded myself to leave at its last station and change to a busier trunk line. Passengers thinned out. The train then halted for a long time. I looked around and was surprised to discover I was the only one left. The overhead light went off. *Poof!* The car was inside a dark maintenance garage, a rusted metal structure, eerily silent, sitting next to other empty trains. A cold breeze brushed my face. I panicked. The doors didn't move. Tears blurred the dark space.

I felt deserted. I didn't know what to do. *Will I join the ranks of war orphans abandoned with tattered clothes and no adult supervision?*

After a while, a conductor in a cap and uniform came down the aisle with a flashlight. I inhaled and wiped tears with the back of my right hand. I looked down at my dangling foot, tightened my body, and was ready to be punished for the crime. I don't recall what he said, but I accepted his gently offered hand. Soon, I was in a sparse-looking police station, where young officers entertained me with candies. The night fell outside. A lone streetlamp cast an orange glow on the gravel pavement.

I must have worn a small white patch on my breast with my name and home address printed, a habit from the air raid during the War. No home had telephones yet. A policeman bicycled to reach my parents. My mother and father arrived on their bicycles past midnight to retrieve me.

When my mother rushed to hug me, I don't recall what my facial expression looked like, perhaps a sheepish smile for joy.

I felt relieved she didn't reprimand me. The cool night breeze caressed my cheeks while I rode in the back seat of my father's bicycle, holding onto his rounded back. •

Copyright 2024, Akira Odani

Akira Odani lives in the ancient city of St. Augustine, Florida. He belongs to Taste Life Twice Writers and the Florida Writers Association. Born in Tokyo, he had written extensively for the Japanese media. Still, more recently, his interest has turned to writing in English and subjects related to his experiences interacting with the two cultures. Some of his work has appeared in the pages of FWA anthologies, *The Weekly Avocet*, PSPP, *Twists and Turns, Lost & Found, Sooner or Later*, and *Now or Never*. He stays active, meditating, swimming, and playing pickleball.

# Rum Punch and Reefers
## by Arlene Mandell

Flinging caution to the winds, I told myself, *Oh, what the hell—go be one of the guys!*

The four sales guys had invited me to join them on the private beach of the luxury hotel we were booked at for a week-long stay in Jamaica. We had just arrived from Miami with our publisher to gather information and to sell ads for a tourist guide. Wild tales of the guys' weekend binges back home did not rattle me. From 9-to-5 they were a friendly bunch who often dropped by my room to bum some Excedrin from the big bottle I kept handy for staff.

Jerry, our graphic designer, had tagged along with the guys. Jerry, whose exceptional skills were in high demand, had been recruited at great expense from New York City. Since our small office had not yet jumped into the digital age, Jerry had to deliver the raw materials personally and review them with the printer, whose shop was in the maze of downtown Miami. Included were voluminous pages of hard copy, plus photographic slides taken on location by the publisher, meticulously labeled and captioned. Jerry tended to detour along the way, arriving late and with materials missing or in disarray. The furious printer threatened to cut off ties with us, despite our company being a longtime customer with multiple products.

As the company proofreader and research editor, I was a solid, strait-laced, all-business employee. I had to be. I supported myself and my mother, with whom I lived. Consequently, the publisher asked me to accompany Jerry. During these back-and-forth drives, Jerry poured out his problems, including a decades-long predilection for drugs, on which he had spent thousands. Nevertheless, sensing a softer side beneath the grittier edges, I grew fond of him. He, in turn, became gentle and protective towards me.

Now I was on my own in Jamaica with the guys from the office. They had formed a circle in the enticing turquoise water lapping the deserted end of the beach, motioning me to join them. There we stood, each of us with rum punch in one hand, passing around "reefers" (aka "weed") with the other. I was not into that stuff but longed to be part of the group.

*Reefers out in the open? Bad idea!* We could have wound up in the local jail. Was this a devil-may-care side of me I did not recognize, or just the Appleton Rum coursing happily through my unsullied veins? As we all returned to the hotel for dinner with the publisher, Jerry teased that reefers were kid stuff. "I have connections here," he promised. "Come to my room after dinner and experience the real thing—*ganja!*"

My options for that evening's entertainment were listening to the publisher talk business with the hotelier, staying alone in my room, or hanging out with the guys and checking out the *ganja*—whatever that was.

Mellow and merry, off I went like Little Red Riding Hood to Jerry's room with the guys. Jerry, now ecstatic, produced the *ganja*, lit up, inhaled deeply, and passed it around our group of greenhorns. Since the bout at the beach had not affected me, I assumed this would not either and took a puff each time the *ganja* came around. I experienced nothing but noticed the normally chatty guys becoming abnormally quiet. Something was happening. My panicky gut sent up red flares!

Recent remarks overheard about *ganja* popped into mind: it could change your personality or make you paranoid. Alarmed, I turned to Jerry, my protector; he was zonked out on the bed. Eight steely eyes stared at me in menacing silence. Bolting like a bat-out-of-hell past the gauntlet of guys, I flew to my room, locked the door, hit the bed running, dove into sleep. I thought I was safe, but then the *ganja* kicked in. Grotesque hallucinations—beyond the pale of ordinary nightmares—hurtled through my brain at high speed in rapid succession.

I woke up gasping for air. It was morning. The phantoms of the night had vanished into oblivion, except for one odd, out-of-place, comical image of elephants sitting in teacups. That singular souvenir became my warning to put the kibosh on mind-altering substances. After that I kept to myself, returning stateside with staff the following week to begin production.

Jerry's guilt at having abandoned me to the wolves was evidenced by a massive purchase of every known vitamin bottle from A to Z, lined up like little soldiers on the shelves of his graphics room. "I'm turning over a new leaf," he declared apologetically. *Uh-huh*. We continued driving together to the printer, making sure nothing got lost along the way. The only thing that *had* gotten lost was my better judgment.

None of the guys mentioned *ganja* again. They continued to bum my Excedrin. •

Copyright 2024, Arlene Mandell

Arlene Mandell is an artist living in Linville, North Carolina, proudly celebrating her 11th year at Carlton Gallery in Banner Elk. (carlton-gallery.com/arlene-mandell). A native New Yorker, relocating to the Blue Ridge Mountains with Captain Dan ignited a passion to write. Her "6-minute Stories" podcasts include: "Eye of the Dolphin," "Artist Borne," "Gobsmacked in the Gulfstream," "Renegade Daughter," "It Started with a Typo," "Shopping for the Homeless," "Thirteen Candles in the Dark," "The Promise of Romance," "At Five & Ninety-Five, Mother Was a Star," "In the Heart of Trauma," "The Jig Is Up," and "Getting a Head Start."

# When I Was a Yard Dog
## by David Lusk

With the rigid plastic band inside my construction-worker hard hat wrenched tight around my skull, my head bobbled with the added weight as I walked down the hill toward the unknown. In the summer of 1973, I was a drop-out seeking refuge from a wild and wooly college campus life infused with the combined mix of psychoactive drugs and mind-numbing alcohol. The first, best, critical decision in my young life had come—to find my way home, to heal, to piece my scattered adolescent sense of self back together.

Too many things had gone wrong, some tragic, in the big city from which I fled. I did have a plan and a dream fueled by hope but mostly idealistic naïveté—make enough money to buy a van, go to California, somehow find "my people," a mystical tribe of nomadic spirits, reach a place where, I believed, there were girls like Joni Mitchell and the music evoked the soulfulness of Ritchie Havens singing "Freedom" at Woodstock. I knew there was such a place, somewhere far out there, far from the looming, cranking, grinding asphalt plant made of gray painted steel, looking ominously steampunk and industrial with tall ladders, silos, gears, valves and conveyor belts. Walking down the hill that morning toward my new job meant entering another world far removed from college English classes, psychology exams, a typewriter, and hours in the library. I thought of Frodo approaching Mordor in J.R.R. Tolkien's Lord of the Rings trilogy, my favorite books at the time.

While daunted, I was, at first, relieved and glad to be in the blue-collar work force and away from school. But having long hair, patched jeans, and wire-rim glasses in the South as late as 1973, years after the culturally catalytic San Francisco "Summer of Love" movement, still communicated a type of radicalism shunned by a conservative, establishment majority. While thankful to have landed a job, I was by job description referred to as the lowly "yard dog." I worked 12-hour days. The first of my many daily tasks was to go inside a tunnel where a conveyor belt moved sand to another part of the plant. I pulled out any excess fallen sand with a large wooden hoe-like tool and then wheelbarrowed the sand out of the tunnel. Most of my time was spent greasing the near-countless moving parts of the plant.

I had much to prove—that a skinny, hungry-for-experience, long-haired college kid could work like hell, stand up to the scorching summer heat, and maybe earn a modicum of respect. These were tough, mostly mean-spirited, working-class dudes that I encountered. The big boss was a fair, no-nonsense old man who would show up when the state inspectors came to test the quality of the asphalt which could then be fashioned into the black ribbon roads that would stretch far into the horizon, all the while, also providing my future escape route to the West, into a fantasy realm of Tolkien's Rivendell of forests and waterfalls far removed from the dust and grime of present realities.

One day a truck delivering bitumen, the hot, black tar used in making asphalt, spilled some accidently. The order from the air-conditioned control tower went out over the plant speakers for the "yard dog" to clean up the spill. Some of it had spread under one of the dozens of conveyor belts. Cleanup required me to use a small pickaxe while on my hands and knees to pry up the thickened tar and then throw the pieces bit by bit into a wheelbarrow. Along with the fifth or fiftieth firmly resounding hammer blow with my pickaxe came a thunderbolt moment of clarity born of every slight, every wound, I had until then ever known. I neither looked down nor looked back that day when I stood up, dropped my pickaxe, and walked up that hill for the last time, stronger, healthier, with a newfound sense of resilience and self-respect. No longer willing to be the lowly yard dog, I most self-assuredly quit the job, confident and fearless in what the future may hold. Then and there, my one hot, dusty summer as a "yard dog" had ended forever.

I did manage to buy an old van, a 1963 Ford Econoline and with $200 in my bitumen-stained jeans pocket was ready to ride west. As much as I loved her, she was not up to the task as my long-sought, freely wondering, tin can, hippie van broke down before I could make it across the country, actually, not even out of town. But a good yard dog perseveres, works hard, is loyal to self and others. Flash forward a mere 50 years later, almost to the day, I made it to Big Sur, California, my Rivendel, at the right time, in the right place, in the right van with the right one by my side. •

*When I Was a Yard Dog*

Copyright 2024, David Lusk

David Lusk is a retired, self-employed consulting arborist/psychologist/writer living in Winston-Salem, North Carolina. He has previously written several articles for the *Winston-Salem Journal* and the trade publication, *Tree Care Industry Magazine*. He lives purposefully in a beech tree woodland with his wife Amy, their two adopted rescue shelter dogs, Jessie Girl, Captain Spaghetti Jack, and Maple Tree the cat. He is currently attempting to create a Japanese garden while under the constant, playful supervision of Jessie and Jack.

# Dismissed

by Annette L. Brown

The athletic director fails to stand when he shakes my extended hand. He fails to invite me to sit.

I sit anyway and glance at the shelf above his head—trophies gathered in previous decades, topped in Vegas-shiny, Lombardy-posed figures. Mr. Olivaris retired from coaching six years prior, in 1980, to become the athletic director.

"Do you have a minute?" My clear eyes peer into his age-clouded grays.

"Yup." He relaxes into his black leather desk chair, hands steepled before him.

"Coach Williams and his basketball athletes interrupted volleyball practice today. I asked them to leave the gym. They didn't." My head throbs with frustration and the echo of basketballs pounding the gym floor.

He regards me down the angle of his nose. "Humm. Sweetheart, I think Coach Williams got under your skin."

"My practice is closed."

"The program is legendary. Hell, he's a legend. It's gotta be intimidating."

I hide my thoughts behind a closed-lip smile and imagine
*Dismissed*

squeezing his smirk between my forefinger and thumb. "I am not intimidated."

"Darlin,' that's a champion—"

"I appreciate his success."

"-ship team. They have tra-di-tions." He pronounces traditions as if I might not recognize the syllable breaks.

*Did the man really just pronounce at me? He needs to leave the '50s and join the post-Title IX era—we're over 10 years in!* I work to unclench my jaw. "The girls deserve their time. I'm not expecting anything special."

"You're seeing red!"

I am feeling red—hot cheeks, boiling headache. "The course catalog lists volleyball practice from 2 to 4 pm in the gym."

"Williams has entered the gym at 3:30 for years."

"I feel compelled to honor the course catalog." *Is my voice too sarcastic? I am tempted to bat my eyes at him.*

His glance brushes toward the wall clock. "Of course, Young Lady."

*Young?— What does that make him? "Old Man"?* Sweat drops from the wispy curls lining the base of my ponytail; it slides down my neck. "I consider the course catalog a contract with our community—that a class will be held at a certain time in a certain place."

"A contract?" He chuckles. "That's a bit much."

"The time is allocated specifically for women's volleyball."

"And volleyball's in there—"

"But—"

"... with a little company." He winks, offers a half smile.

I ignore both. "Your head women's volleyball coach is asking you to support her request for a closed practice." I slide both hands over my hair to keep back the renegade straggler curls, a tension habit leftover from my days as a competitor.

He raises his right brow. "You really wanna be the new girl who comes in here and rocks the boat?"

The late afternoon sun peeking through his office window catches the silver shine of his hair. That shine and the sting of "girl" blur my vision. He judges me as some upstart, 20-something who doesn't know her place. I want to retort, *Don't threaten me.* But why would I say that? Of course, he can threaten me. Even the previous volleyball coach of eight years, who was a man, allowed the "tra-di-tion." But why? Because the basketball program is "legendary"? I bite the inside of my lip. I should keep my mouth shut. No boat rocking. I know it would be the smart thing to do. But I just—can't. I shake my head. Oh well, one year of a college-level head coaching position is something.

"Two hours—undisturbed. Please." I train my eyes on his. Turning away would feel too much like surrender. He has power. I have resolve. *Does resolve ever win?*

Eyes fixed on me, he adjusts his hands, places the fingernail of one thumb beneath the nail of the other and flicks. Flick, flick, flick. He glances at the clock. Little knots of tension tighten my shoulders.

I attempt a Hail Mary: "Over half my athletes are freshmen

*Dismissed*

and unfamiliar with at least one skill or play I'm covering. This naturally creates some anxiousness. They don't need an audience to exacerbate that."

"Ex-aaa-cerbate. You do like your $10 words." He shakes his head, then glancing at the clock again, stands, and walks around the desk.

Hands balled into fists, I stand. His hand on my lower back, he guides me to the door. "I'll see what I can do."

I fight not to flinch at his touch. "Thank you." Sure, he'll talk to Coach Williams. They'll have a beer and a good laugh at this barely-out-of-college newbie "girl" who expects to make changes.

As I regard his 60-something stride, the scream fighting to escape my throat dissolves into a plan. I'll give Mr. Olivaris one day. Then this *Young Lady—Sweetheart—Girl* will take her concern to his boss, the dean overseeing athletics, a woman, who may be more interested in giving female athletes their due.

Turns out, she is. •

Copyright 2024, Annette L. Brown

Annette L. Brown is a mother, wife, and retired teacher, who lives on an almond farm in Central California where she enjoys spending time with family and friends. She is grateful for the support of The Taste Life Twice Writers and The Light Makers' Society and for simply having time to write. Annette has pieces reflecting her love of nature, family, beauty, and humor in several publications including *Pictura Journal, Last Stanza Poetry, Flash Fiction Magazine, Every Day Fiction,* and other PSP Project anthologies.

# Naked Relief
## by Jena Reger

I tossed my bikini on the white sand bank above the dark water to prove to myself that I was fully committed to swimming naked and had no reservations about the choice I'd made. The midnight saltwater was cool and inviting, and I didn't take any time to consider that I'd just left my bathing suit on a public beach.

It was the night of June 7, 1997—my best friend's 16th birthday. Lily, let's call her, only lived blocks from Manasota Key Beach, and our birthday party squad of teenage girls had decided to go skinny dipping. Lily had regaled us with tales of swimming at night off the beach and witnessing the bioluminescence of dinoflagellates (mostly marine plankton). She had taken off her bathing suit to unsettle the water and watch the sparkling blue light of living organisms. That's how you see the bioluminescence—when the water is disturbed by waves—or thrashing bikinis.

Hopeful to recreate this transcendent experience, our posse of girls decided that a late-night dip in the Gulf of Mexico was in order. I can't remember who suggested that we go skinny dipping that night. I probably did. I had a certain *joie de vivre* at 16—I could drive a car, my hair was finally growing out after a horrific haircut at the beginning of my sophomore year, and life was teeming with possibilities. I couldn't think of a better way to celebrate Lily's birthday than to swim in the nude.

All but one of us decided to take the naked plunge. For whatever reason, Grace refused to go skinny dipping despite our protracted nagging. After I was in the water, I was oblivious to what was happening on the beach. The saltwater caressed my bare skin and felt sublime. The moonlight was dim, and the powdery, white sand stood in bold relief against the dark water. The salty and humid air felt soft against my wet skin, and I squealed in delight as schools of small fish brushed up against my ankles. The ultimate freedom of swimming naked simultaneously exhilarated and soothed my senses. I was completely unrestricted from the binding elastic and spandex of my bikini, and I delighted in the way that the waves lapped against my small bare breasts. The horrific and very real possibility of sharks feeding close offshore late at night never crossed my mind. I would only learn about this later.

Meanwhile, back on the beach, Grace ran into some high school boys up to no good. She was pissed at us for pressuring her to go skinny dipping and told them what we were doing. Some of us, me included, had thrown caution to the wind—and our bathing suits on the beach. Others, perhaps wiser, were clutching their swimsuits in their hands in the water, when the boys appeared. With great delight, the guys laughed loudly as they stole our swimwear and towels.

Panic set in. In an age before cell phones were ubiquitous, I imagined a veritable walk of shame back to Lily's house, fittingly, in our birthday suits. We yelled at the boys to leave us alone. They only laughed at us. We huddled close together as we moved farther offshore to obscure our nakedness. Grace must have known these boys because it was apparent that nothing more nefarious than a high school prank was at play. It was clear they only wanted to steal our clothes, not come into the water with us. Plus, we outnumbered them, six girls to only three boys.

Something must have shifted for Grace. After only a minute of their antics, she went from inciting the situation to threatening the boys if they did not return our bikinis. Grace was a soccer player and extremely fit. She also brooked no nonsense. Apparently regretting her earlier decision to tell them about our clandestine activity, she became our protector. Sparring with Grace physically or verbally was a bad idea. She marched up to the ringleader, ready to unload. Whatever she threatened to do to them, it was evident they believed she could—and would. The boys relented immediately, handed over the swimsuits and slinked away.

The showdown with the boys on Manasota Beach was enough to squash our desire for adventure and the quest for bioluminescence. We bandied about a few ideas, but ultimately decided that going home was the best option.

Despite my brush with unimaginable teenage embarrassment, I did go skinny dipping again, but I did not foolishly leave my suit on the sand. In defense of my 16-year-old self, though, tossing caution to the wind that night produced the better memories. •

*Naked Relief*

Copyright 2024, Jena Reger

Jena Reger lives in Durham, North Carolina, where she is a graduate student at Duke University. She belongs to a local writing group and has been working on a variety of projects for the past few years--from flash fiction to a novel. Her work has appeared in the online literary magazine *Swamp Biscuits and Tea* and the anthology, *Coming of Age in Florida*.

# Open Mouth, Insert Footlong Garden Hose
## by Nick Sipe

"The cows made me do it. They made me drink gasoline."

I might have uttered those words, but I was too busy coughing, crying, trying to vomit, and trying not to vomit, unsure which was best.

This was 1992. I was 13. My parents left me home alone because I'd become mature. Responsible. Or so we all thought. No one had cell phones, so in an emergency, you settled for whomever was at home if you were too cowardly to call 911.

"Hello?" Mamaw crowed, nearly deaf and already blind.

"It's me," I croaked.

"Who is this?" No caller ID then either.

"Your grandson. I drank gasoline!"

"Why'd you want to do that for?" *You durn fool* was implied at the end of that question, but her bless-your-heart manners forbid her saying it.

What happened after was a blur, but what came before that phone call is clear in my memory.

Lying in a sea of blue shag carpet, sketching superheroes in the floor because pencils were forbidden on my waterbed, a *Mooooo!* erupted from outside my bedroom window. We lived in rural North Carolina, but we didn't own cows. Our relatives did. Our neighbors did, but my family was *cow-adjacent*.

The cow-adjacent know only two things about cows:
1. Don't step in the patties.
2. Never share a cow with family.

Out my window, two cows grazed quietly in our backyard, and I knew why. We had spent that summer replacing a barbwire fence with chain link. Before each new section was built, we cut and removed the barbwire. Two days before, a popup shower forced us to abandon our work, leaving a gap in the fence the exact width of a cow.

High on a newfound sense of independence, I decided I should act swiftly. Decisively. Oh, how my parents would beam hearing how I'd herded the cows away single-handedly. A real cowboy would use a horse, but the closest thing we had was a Yamaha four-wheeler. In my mind, the Yamaha had a certain modern nobility.

Sadly, the four-wheeler was out of gas. As was the can in the garage. How could I get gas? Hadn't I watched my old man, a shade tree mechanic, use an orange hose with a pump to siphon gas from one vehicle to another? I searched in vain for the siphon hose but never found it.

Instead, I found a footlong piece of garden hose and a riding lawnmower with a full tank of gas. Serendipitously, the mower was parked next to the four-wheeler! Using the hose, I could simply pump gasoline from one into the other. With a small amount of suction, the gas would flow seamlessly.

I positioned the footlong piece of hose over the mower's gas tank. A small puff would get the gas flowing, and then I'd divert the gas safely to the four-wheeler. I exhaled all the air from my lungs, so that I might get strong suction. In retrospect, I probably looked like a kid settling down to the world's most unappealing milkshake.

I never got a chance to divert the gasoline, as my strong suction pulled large mouthfuls straight into my mouth. My mouth flooded with gasoline, I instinctively swallowed instead of spitting it out. Waves of hot lava washed down my throat, past my lungs, and hit my stomach like an acid avalanche. The burning was intense and the smell of gasoline everywhere, like I had bathed in it.

I was in serious trouble.

Worrying I'd poisoned myself, my frenzied mind could think of no way to contact Poison Control, so I called Mamaw. *Durn fool* or no, she called Poison Control while I waited for what felt like hours for her to call me back. Poison Control prescribed lots of water and eating Rolaids one after another to neutralize the acid in my stomach. I was on my second pack of Rolaids when my parents arrived. The rest is a blur. I only remember my urine and tears reeking like a gas station.

*Open Mouth, Insert Footlong Garden Hose*

Adding insult to injury, the cows mooed all night. Taunting me.

The next day the only lingering effects were a sore throat and stomach. Poison Control suspected I had first degree chemical burns on my esophagus and stomach lining that would heal normally over time.

My father called his Uncle Joe, a *cow-owner*, who always wore blue coveralls and an easy smile. Joe proclaimed he knew how to get the cows back to their pasture. I pictured a bullhorn, a well-trained dog, or Joe on a four-wheeler, but in the end, he only brought a handful of straw.

Casually walking past the cows, Joe let them sniff the straw and they simply followed him back to their pasture.

Life in the country is hard, especially for durn fools and the cow-adjacent. •


Copyright 2024, Nick Sipe

By day, Nick Sipe works as a mild-mannered IT manager for a Fortune 150 company. By night, he mostly recovers from the workday, but occasionally finds time to write. He enjoys writing Twilight Zone-style short stories, mostly horror and light sci-fi. Nick is currently shopping his debut novel, "Midnight Springs," to literary agents. "Midnight Springs" is the first in a planned horror-Western series that sends classic monsters (think Frankenstein, Van Helsing, the Wolfman) to the Wild West to tangle with their American counterparts (think witches, the Headless Horseman, the Wendigo).

# Eavesdropping
## by Eloise Currie

From the time I was 9 years old, I knew our life was crumbling. As I grew, so did my awareness of my parents' constant disagreements and the increasing distance between them. Conversation shut down when I approached. Faces pinched, they resumed arguing when they thought I could not hear. Dad traveled and, when home, he barely acknowledged me. Mom was busy constructing their social life, which consisted of cocktail parties and did not include families with children. Interaction with me was sporadic. I was a trespasser, always underfoot.

Desperate to understand why things were going wrong, I began a stealthy search for clues. Dad drank and, too drunk to reason, was not making the best choices for stashing bottles. Why would he be interested in the linen closet contents or inspecting the workings of the toilet tank? When Mom caught him, he provided furious, nonsensical explanations, his voice fuzzy from alcohol.

"Makin' funny noise," he yelled when caught, having enunciation problems. His anger was pervasive. She pushed the handle, and it flushed just fine. I found him frightening and admired the courage it took her to confront him.

Knowing his hiding places was not enough. I had to know what was being said when they thought I was not around. The meaningful conversations took place after I went to bed. Loud but unintelligible voices drifted up the stairs into my room. Standing at my door to listen seemed safe enough.

But I could only hear snatches, not full sentences. I abandoned safety at my bedroom door and crept to the top of the stairs. Bare feet silent on the carpet, I was certain I could just make it back to bed without being heard and look realistically asleep should Mom decide to come up to check on me. She did this on occasion, which added to my nerves. I knew this because, due to their arguments, I never slept well.

With my heart hammering, I discovered things about our lack of money, debts, and Dad's affair, something I had never heard of but about which I soon learned too much. Dad's muttered half-answers to Mom's anxious questions were difficult to understand, but what he said was what I needed to hear. Maybe another stair down would be doable. Two became three. I could hear furniture creaking, a warning that one of them was getting up, my signal to fly to my room.

I couldn't quit. What I heard was important to know and I had to continue this risky addiction to their conversations. Narrow escapes were not enough to frighten me into stopping. Thoughts about what I was doing began to occupy my days, filling them with anxiety. Would this be the night I would risk four steps down, almost within view of Mom's chair, likely out of the range of safety?

One night, I became the topic of their conversation. They discussed me at length. I was stunned to learn that I was generally lacking in everything. Not getting straight A's. Not helping enough around the house, though I did everything they asked. Criticized for not loving the new dog, an unmanageable creature they had brought home from the animal shelter when my beloved collie had been hit and killed. Feeling that they could not come home empty-handed with bad news, they had scooped up a dog from the shelter. Unplug old dog, plug in new; a dog was a dog. I was labeled ungrateful for not loving it and criticized for crying about my collie. But they had done their parental duty, they said.

"Honey, what would you like to name your new dog?"
When I could not answer, Mom had the solution.

"Let's name the new dog 'Happy'." I was stunned; she could not have made a more ill-advised choice. Happy it was from then on.

Confused and shaking, I went back up the stairs, forgetting the one squeaky board. Conversation stopped. Couch and chair creaked in unison. Petrified, I made it to my door, hearing two sets of footsteps on the stairs.

I burrowed under covers, head on pillow with mouth open slightly, breathing lightly, arm flung out, all hopefully convincing. The door opened, hinges squeaking. Mom came over to peer closely at me which seemed to take hours. I prayed she didn't notice my shaking. I was dying to take a deep breath.

*Eavesdropping*

"Look at her. She's dead asleep," she whispered. They left, closing the door firmly. I gasped for air. Finally, an end.

But there would be no end. I could not trust them or feel safe. I did not feel wanted. Life was washed with grey, and anxiety and depression blossomed in my brain and stayed with me. I learned that once knowing something, it is impossible to un-know it. I was wiser about the goings-on but stunned into deep sadness and gut-wrenching anxiety.

Had it been worth it? It was not a foolish mistake. I never regretted what I did. Ignorance would have been more intolerable than knowing. Afterward, I had a road map for the rest of my childhood.

The trips down the stairs became unnecessary. •

Copyright 2024, Eloise Currie

Eloise Currie lives in Raleigh, North Carolina. She has kept a journal for thirty years and uses it as source material for short stories and nonfiction. She lived in Bath, North Carolina, for several years where she was a member of the Pamlico Writers Group and Riverwalk Writers Group. She is currently a member of the River Writers Group. She enjoys editing and has edited two books as well as short pieces.

# A Hundred Percent
## by Lisa Williams Kline

When we asked the delightful young Justin-Timberlake-lookalike who sold us our new electric car if we could make it to our beach house for Christmas without stopping to charge, he said "A hundred percent!"

"A hundred percent!" Jeff repeated as we climbed into our brand-new EV for that first 200-mile drive to the coast. "The dashboard says we can go 240 miles."

"Forty miles to spare," I agreed.

We'd loaded our suitcases, Jeff's golf clubs, his guitar, and all the holiday gifts for our daughters and their husbands into the car, since we would be hosting Hanukkah and Christmas at the beach in a week. We'd also loaded our pet carriers with Joni, our sweet chihuahua and Lionman, our high-maintenance cat.

We followed our well-worn route, enjoying the new car smell, and the nearly silent hum of our electric engine, feeling like The Jetsons. While Jeff drove, I played with the climate controls, and tried to find NPR.

I found a few chargers along the way in the unlikely event we'd need one. As we drove, I watched the dashboard to see how quickly our range was shrinking. Suddenly, I didn't like what I was seeing.

"Jeff," I said. "Our range just shrunk by 20 miles. But we couldn't have gone more than five. The speed that the range is shrinking doesn't correlate with the actual number of miles we've driven."

"That's impossible," Jeff said. "When we left, we had 240 miles on our battery. We can make it to the beach."

"It's already down to 170 and we've only gone about 30 miles. We're going to have to stop and charge."

"We're not doing it!"

I quietly got out our car manual. In small print, a paragraph explained that EV mileage is variable dependent upon how heavily the car is loaded as well as cold temperatures. In winter our vehicle could get up to 30 percent less mileage. Thirty percent!

Just then, a message came up on our dashboard.

"You do not have enough charge to get to your destination. Would you like to add a charging station to your route?"

"Should I agree?"

"No, we're not stopping! Just ignore it!" Jeff growled, his hands tight on the steering wheel. I was reminded of that old Seinfeld episode where Kramer was trying to reach some destination by driving on fumes, insanely determined to test the limits of his gas tank.

I tapped the screen to dismiss the warning. We drove ten more miles and I watched our range drop by 25.

I ground my teeth, my hands turned cold, and my chest felt tight. I now know that I was in the throes of a new phenomenon—range anxiety. Since gas stations greatly outnumber charging stations, even when you do find a charger, it may not be available, so EV highway drivers can be in a constant state of anxiety.

The warning came on the dashboard again.

"Jeff, we have to stop."

"I'm getting rid of this car!" he shouted. "This is not what we signed up for!"

I found a charger a short distance off the highway, in front of a local electric utility headquarters. We plugged in, after much fumbling with the apps and the charger. We ate lunch. We walked Joni. Jeff took a long walk to let off steam. The people in the headquarters let us use their restrooms. The only one who got no relief was Lionman, who crouched bravely in his carrier.

We'd accidentally stopped at a slow charger, though, so, after two frustrating hours, we took a chance on a fast charger I found nearby that would get the job done in 45 minutes. We exited the highway and saw the single charger sitting off in a corner of a gas station. Hallelujah, no one else was using it! I almost fainted with relief.

"Charge to 100 percent!!" I told Jeff. Once back on the road, I called "Justin Timberlake," our car salesman.

"Justin, can we return this car?"

"No, I'm sorry, your three-day right of rescission is over."

*A Hundred Percent*

"You told us we could make it to the beach without charging. But we just had to stop and charge twice. A trip that used to take us four hours is going to take seven."

"Well," he said. "It's pretty cold today. That affects how well your car can hold its charge."

Now you tell us.

"So, when it's warm weather, we'll be able to make it to the beach without charging?"

"A hundred percent!" Justin said.

At dusk, exhausted, we pulled, into the driveway at our beach house with about 40% charge left on our battery and two stoic pets.

"Whew, ready for a drink?" Jeff said.

"A hundred percent!"

Foolhardy not to do more research? Yes.

Foolhardy to do the right thing? Not at all. •

Copyright 2024, Lisa Williams Kline

Lisa Williams Kline is the author of two award-winning novels for adults, *Between the Sky and the Sea* and *Ladies' Day*, as well as an essay collection entitled *The Ruby Mirror* and a short story collection entitled *Take Me*. She lives in Davidson with her veterinarian husband, a cat who can open doors, and a sweet chihuahua who has played Bruiser Woods in *Legally Blonde: The Musical*.

# No Stopping To Think
## by Thomas Gery

Was it foolhardy to help my mother die?

In the late 1940's with the Boomer Generation in its infancy, I was spanked into the world of life and breath. The August temperature outside was 95 degrees. The hospital room had only a fan. After hours of anguish, prayers whispered, curses screamed, my 22-year-old mother delivered her first born. She would go on to deliver two more sons, 15 and 19 years later. In between she adopted her second son when I was 8. Mary, herself the first of six, named after that most blessed of women, was draped with a mantel of responsibility.

In March 2008 the surgeon ordered hospice. A left breast mastectomy several years prior was not followed up with a normal course of radiation and chemotherapy. Mom had her own ideas. Now a golf-ball-size lump in her remaining breast signaled cancer's return.

Mary was born during the roaring 20's to working class city folks who believed in the American Dream. They met as workers in a knitting mill; silk stockings were high fashion. The colonial village on the Schuylkill River had become a midsize industrial town. Corruption, clandestine breweries, gambling and prostitution, along with blind eyes of local officials are documented in criminology textbooks. Mom's father ran a card game in the back room of the family candy store. A hard worker, he used business acumen and well-earned capital to open a neighborhood bar and restaurant. My grandmother was in the kitchen, Mom waiting tables.

Grandfather was a stern patriarch. As an adolescent, Mary missed a year of school to stay home with her sick mother and young siblings. The Catholic school principal waived the attendance requirement. Mom's self-confidence suffered a setback.

Twenty-year-old Mary was given away by a domineering father to a demanding groom, himself, steeped in the culture of women as second-class citizens. With her raven black hair, innocent brown eyes, ivory complexion, and welcoming smile she received attention as a waitress. Twice her own preference of suitor was overruled. The status conscious patriarch thought my father's name bespoke wealth and a higher social circle.

Mom believed marriage was a life-long commitment. After years of strife, long absences with hints of unfaithfulness, my father got his way with a 1995 divorce. Five years earlier my youngest brother, age 22, was killed in a motorcycle accident. Health wise, diabetes and hypertension ganged up on her.

Mom had to become independent of the husband who for almost 50 years filled a traditional role. I watched her learn to manage meager finances, keep her car running, cut the lawn.

Since before divorce, I was Mom's backstop. She would reluctantly signal a rising anxiety level: "Tom, I'm in trouble." Was I being foolhardy by not stopping to think before making a promise? Relationships can be changed, sometimes harmed by stress; the dying process is a crucible of tension. I committed to Mom; she would die in her own space, not an institution.

Stress stalked me: work obligations at the dialysis clinic; spouse living five hours south in our future home; a sick, old, pet dog; my beloved mother dying. Medicare Hospice was billed 123 days. The end is recorded in agency staff notes, my journal and memory.

> Good start, likes staff - periodic aches, pain - hurts to breathe - tries morphine - attends grand daughter's baby shower - 44 days into service - accepts minimum pain meds - Last Sacrament received - we talk, we cry - she stubbornly says being alone is ok - still performing activities of daily living - family visiting on weekends - day 62 of service, private duty aid begins - day 69 mom holds first great grandchild, radiates joy from a dying face - day 74 bed sores developing, her 82nd birthday - open mouth breathing, air hunger, O2 declined - some pain meds accepted, cancer metastasized, severe bone pain, nausea, vomiting - day 93 weaker by the day, accepts some meds, hallucinations - day 104 agony, resistance, debilitation, the smell of a cancerous wound - day 123 pronounced dead.

Near the end we talked, shed tears; she tired quickly. Mom said, "I know what is coming," I asked why she often resisted medication, pain relieving morphine, fentanyl patches, Compazine. One word came—*suffering*. Then I knew.

*No Stopping To Think*

She suffered through my birth for a good end in a hospital room on a hot August day. Mom suffered now to get home to her own mother and youngest son. Pain meds would prolong the journey. Mary had a heart of gold and a Catholic soul.

I had not been foolhardy. Mom carried me, birthed me, loved a helpless, dependent human being. She gave me her all. There was no stopping to think. It was instinct. It was meant to be. •

Copyright 2024, Thomas Gery

Thomas Gery, a common man with uncommon experiences lives in Berks County, Pennsylvania. He served in the U.S. Army with duty in Vietnam. As a social worker he helped children, youth, and adults in a variety of practice venues and situations throughout a work life of 40 years. Married with two adult children and two grandchildren, he is currently writing his life's story to provide answers to questions his kids will never ask. His earlier published stories have appeared in Personal Story Publishing Project—*Lost & Found*, *Sooner or Later*, and *Now or Never*.

# Williams Adventures
## by Ginny Foard

In 2024's winter chill, I aimlessly browse maps. I remember an old diary about going to Scotland. I feel that I want to walk on a patch of dirt, in a country I've never been to. Why? A foolish whim?

Long ago, this same dirt beckoned to another. His diary begins, "On the seventh of March 1833 I left my native town with a heart rejoicing." Twenty-four-year old William Augustus Williams says he's "to undertake a journey ... so long contemplated ... of seeing the land of my forefathers and an aged grandmother. Yet a little grieved at parting with my mother who was much averse to my journey I set out."

William was born and raised in Wilmington, North Carolina. He knew his mother opposed his trip for a good reason.

Years earlier, in 1803, William's father John left home in Scotland. John was 25. His last name was Williamson. By the time his ship landed in Wilmington, John was gravely ill. The port official recorded John's last name as "Williams." John accepted the error without protest, believing he would soon be dead anyway.

John was made of strong stuff, though. Two years later, he was still alive, married, and making his way as a commercial merchant. Soon William and other children arrived. John frequently wrote to his mother and brothers in Scotland.

These far-away family and lands enticed William. He saw bustling Wilmington port trade and heard of dangerous high seas. The siren song of the unknown called.

William answered the call, despite his mother's worries. He gathered letters from friends to introduce him to "persons of respectability" in Liverpool, London, Edinburgh, and elsewhere.

His trip's diary begins with a prayer against "the dangers of the sea, from sickness, and from every evil" so that William may return safe to his parents. He was one of five passengers on a packet out of New York to Liverpool. For three weeks, he inked weather, wind, speed and sea conditions. He heard ocean splashes, smelt salt air, saw nightly constellations. He wrote of "studdensails" and "three reefed topsails." He heard the "joyful cry of 'Land O' ... sounded from the fore top."

Traveling from England into Scotland over four more weeks, William finally met his "way worn Grandmother" and aunts in Linlithgow. Drinking health to the king that night, he "was forced to face a large company of strangers in returning thanks and giving a toast in return." He visited nearby places. One day returning by boat to Edinburgh, he accidentally found he had "been along side my friend Mr. Gray all the way. He immediately invited me to his house to dinner." All the while, William attended to business interests and made acquaintances to further his budding commercial career.

After another two weeks, to his "great pleasure and satisfaction" he got a letter from home. Then, enjoying visiting, William noted his "intention to have spent three days with my friend Gregory but find I have stopped ten." Finally, William bade farewell to his "poor old grandmother who parted with me with a sad heart while the tears rolled down her time furrowed cheeks. Her grief was great as in the course of nature we can never expect to meet again in this world." He said goodbye to aunts, uncles and cousins. Some walked miles with him to his next stop. William took the coach for Glasgow, "turning face towards home."

As I peruse maps, I notice an odd art cruise aboard a repurposed rescue boat. The advertisement says guests can use seaweed as a paintbrush while traveling Scotland's Hebrides islands. The only luxury is the view, it says. There's a cancellation—one berth is available. I imagine being on the boat.

I remember William's diary about Scotland. His great-grandson was William Williams Foard, my father. In 1942, William's granddaughter, my father's aunt Helen, gave him a copy.

I find my diary copy. I read that William walked from Glasgow to his "father's birth place four miles on the Cumbernauld road. After a little enquiring and searching [he] found the place White hill." He met an old woman who knew his family.

William's grandfather had built her house. She and her husband worked on his farm. She invited William inside to "crack" (chat).

William wrote he "with a sorrowful heart took my last farewell of Scotia… Never was I more hospitably treated… I found a warmhearted people."

I find Cumbernauld Road on a map. White Hill Farm Road is five miles down the road out of Glasgow. A 2021 Facebook photograph shows a tractor tilling soil on White Hill Farm, with a walker's grateful note that the farmer left a footpath beside the fields.

I am my ancestors' child, foolishness and all.
I book the art boat and tickets to Glasgow. •

Copyright 2024, Ginny Foard

Growing up in the South means hearing and sharing stories. Ginny Foard learned a lot that way and keeps on trying to find out more about it all. The air is thick with good stories. She lives in a little post office box on Sullivans Island, South Carolina.

# Fallout
## by Suzanne Cottrell

The sirens wail through McGuffey Elementary School in Oxford, Ohio. My fourth-grade classmates and I cover our ears and moan. Ms. Carson shouts, "Drop." We jerk our chairs from our desks. We girls brush our hands over our bottoms and tuck our skirts as we kneel, glare at the boys, and crouch under our desks.

Thunk. "Ouch!" Rob rubs his forehead.

Giggles circulate throughout the classroom until *THWACK*; Ms. Carson smacks a ruler on the chalkboard. "The faster everyone gets quiet and in position, the sooner this drill will be over."

We scrunch into balls like armadillos with our fingers clasped over the back of our necks. Minutes creep. I can't see the clock. My legs tingle, and numbness follows. *How much longer?*

"Shh." Ms. Carson patrols between rows of desks before crouching behind hers.

Although my arms and back ache, I can endure a longer drill if Ms. Carson will delay the math lesson on adding and subtracting fractions with unlike denominators.

The siren blast stops. "All clear." Ms. Carson hobbles to the chalkboard and claps her hands. "Time for math."

A wave of soft groans overtakes the silence as we scoot from under our desks and uncurl our bodies. I grasp the sides of my chair, hoist myself on wobbly legs, and plop on the seat.

Although I attempted my homework, I lower my eyes, hoping Ms. Carson will not call on me. The rest of the school day is routine.

Along with fire drills and tornado drills, we practice air raid drills at least once a month. The next morning during the umpteenth viewing of the Civil Defense film, "Duck and Cover," we mimic Bert the Turtle and snicker at the family picnic scene. When a bright light flashes in the sky, the father kneels and covers his head with a newspaper, and the mother and two children hide under a blanket. *If we're having recess, can we scramble to the school's fallout shelter fast enough?*

Miami University of Ohio houses its elementary education lab school in McGuffey Hall, also a designated public bomb shelter. The university's campus is about four miles from a Nike Hercules Missile launch site, northwest of town. When readied, the U.S. Army can launch two-stage guided missiles, towering forty feet, from twelve platforms in fewer than fifteen minutes. Knowing the location of the base, an aggressor's potential target, is not a comfort. *Did government officials expect us to believe a fallout shelter is adequate protection? Hmmm, safe haven or a tomb?*

My dismissive attitude changes to apprehension when our dad stacks cement blocks, forming an oversized closet, in the southwest corner of our musty, cool basement. A fallout shelter is in progress. Using bricks and boards, he constructs shelving. Our mom directs my three siblings and me to stock a shelf with a variety of canned food staples like SPAM®, tuna, peaches, green beans, and other vegetables. My arms ache and my feet drag as I make multiple trips from the kitchen to the basement. We store saltine crackers and vanilla wafers in a small sealable garbage can. Our mom designates a shelf for paper products, plastic utensils, and stainless-steel pots. Another shelf holds a first aid kit, flashlights, matches, and a Sterno camp stove. Blankets, pillows, and sleeping bags lay on a portable cot under which we stow foam pads. Our dad rigs a garbage bag under a toilet seat placed over a bucket. Grimacing, I pray we never have to use it. He insists on having a crank radio to receive important news. Civil Defense officials claim two weeks after an atomic bomb explosion, radiation levels will drop to safe levels, so we can emerge from our basement burrow, assuming we survive living in cramped quarters with bored, bickering family members.

The increased air raid drills at home heighten my insecurity. Blaring sirens, flashes of light, mushroom clouds, and scorched trees and bodies fuel my nightmares. I shriek and wake, clutching my pillow. My mom sits on my bed and rubs my back. She assures me we're safe. I want to believe her. Then she tucks the covers over my shoulders, kisses my forehead, and tiptoes from my bedroom.

*Fallout*

In September 1962, my family moves to the Finger Lakes Region of New York, far removed from a Nike Hercules Missile launch site. Despite missing my friends, I enjoy a brief reprieve from the air raid drills and nightmares until October 16th, with television news coverage of the onset of the Cuban Missile Crisis. Pressing my hands to my temples, *what, no fallout shelter in the basement!* My arms and legs ache, and I brace for a return to interrupted nights' sleep. •

Copyright 2024, Suzanne Cottrell

Suzanne Cottrell, a member of the Taste Life Twice Writers and NC Writers' Network, lives with her husband in rural Granville County, NC. An outdoor enthusiast and retired teacher, she enjoys reading, writing, knitting, hiking, Pilates, and belly dancing. Her prose has appeared in numerous journals and anthologies, including the Personal Story Publishing Project, Inwood Indiana Press, Quillkeepers Press, and *Parks and Points*. She's the author of three poetry chapbooks: *Gifts of the Seasons, Autumn and Winter*; *Gifts of the Seasons, Spring and Summer*; and *Scarred Resilience*; and *Nature Calls Outside My Window, A Collection of Poems and Stories*. www.suzanneswords.com

# A Place To Hang Out
## by Joe Brown

On November 4, 1968, I turned in my excuse for missing school. It stated that I had been "out of town with relatives."

My mother had written and signed it, so it had to be truthful. The assistant principal at the desk looked at the note then back at me, a 16-year-old sophomore. He smiled then quietly asked, "Did you get one?"

"Yes, Sir, sure did!" With his approval I headed back to class. Davie County was a small school, and everyone knew.

The real reason for my week-long absence was a bear-hunting trip to the swamps of Eastern North Carolina. I had been dreaming of this trip with my "relative" (older brother Santford) for months. Other hunters from Mocksville and the mountains of North Carolina had arranged and planned the details of the excursion. The economic situation and time that I grew up in dictated that hunting and fishing were not sports, rather they were survival techniques that were very satisfying—filling the need for both adventure and food.

We lived in a backwoods area of Davie County, North Carolina, the same general area that Daniel Boone (my hero) had moved to when he was a teenager. The county had thousands of acres of Yadkin River bottoms and forested land with few inhabitants. For an aspiring outdoorsman, it was paradise.

My dad had taken me hunting, fishing, and trapping as a youth and by the age of 13, my parents trusted me to take the Stevens 20-gauge double and go hunting for squirrel, rabbit, or quail. At 16, I was a veteran hunter and a pretty good shot.

My weapon of choice for this bear hunt was the same old Stevens 311 20-gauge double. Even with the forearm taped on with electrical tape and a chip off the bottom of the stock, it was very dependable. And I could hit what I aimed at with it. Besides, it was my only gun. That settled the affair. Loaded with rifled slugs, I was certain it would be adequate for Black Bear.

It was early morning October 31 when the standing hunters spread out a hundred yards apart along a canal ditch road. It was cold with a fog-like mist rising from the water of the canal. Hearing a rustle in the thicket across the water I took a couple steps to the edge of the canal. There, about 30 yards down the edge, on the opposite shore, stood the first Black Bear I ever saw. Only its head and front leg were visible but looked like the perfect place to shoot. I quickly put the bead on the target and pulled the trigger. The bear disappeared but by the thrashing around, I could tell I had hit it. Then all was quiet.

When the other hunters came to where I was and I explained all that had transpired, one grizzled old mountain man asked, "How you going to get Your Bear?" On Halloween Day with the temperature in the low 40s, I stripped down to my over-washed, reddish long-johns. The others assured me the water probably wasn't very deep, but when I jumped in, I went plumb out of sight. When I came up, I dog-paddled to the other side. Probably the most foolish thing I'd ever done, to that point, was to jump into that deep black water canal.

One hunter stripped off his holstered 357 revolver, tied it in a ball, and tossed the belt and all to me. Without a doubt the MOST foolish thing I have ever done was stalk around the edge of a jungle with a pistol looking for a wounded bear. They said I was a sight—a six-foot-one-inch, 145-pound boy, wet, pink underwear, gun belt strapped on, poking the pistol into the bushes then taking a step to see if I could find my possibly wounded bear.

We eventually pulled a log across the canal for a foot bridge, where I was joined by some more experienced hunters on my side with the bear. After exploring into the jungle of the drained swamp we found the prey. The trusty 20-gauge had done the job.

For 50 years I had no good place to display my high school trophy. When we built our new house a few years ago, I designed a room for me—a Man Cave. I built a frame for my bearskin rug, hung it behind my recliner. Now we both have a place to hang out.

*A Place To Hang Out*

Youth can entice us to do some crazy things. I sure do miss it! •

Copyright 2024, Joe Brown

Joe Brown is a retired building contractor. He lives on a small family farm in the Bethania area of Winston Salem, North Carolina.
He now has time to do all those projects that a busy work schedule didn't allow. He enjoys his grandchildren and great grandchildren and as time allows likes to reflect on his life and write stories about his adventures. Several of those stories have been shared through the Personal Publishing Project. His prayer is that his family can appreciate the history he has lived.

# You Think You Can Be a Housekeeper
by Evelyn Eickmeyer-Quiñones

Looking back from the mirror was a familiar face in an unfamiliar frock. The black, thigh-length polyester dress with the frilly white collar and apron was a housekeeper's uniform. I did a double take. *Why am I wearing this dress?*

My friends were not surprised when I announced my career change from management to education.

I grew tired of listening to myself talk and finally decided to enroll at Hofstra University on Long Island to earn my master's degree. My current position left me with little energy at the end of the day–I had been commuting into Manhattan for eight years. It had grown old. I needed a new plan if I were going to have the time and energy to study.

The heading "Domestics" shone like a beacon when I began scouring *Newsday*'s Sunday classifieds. *Why not?* I thought. *I know someone who had comfortably retired on their earnings as a housekeeper.* The premise was simple – you see something dirty; you clean it. The more I thought, the more I was convinced. Then the job of my dreams appeared.

*You Think You Can Be a Housekeeper*

"Experienced Housekeeper for Chief Financial Officer's house. Excellent fringe benefits."

The word *experienced* frightened me, but I trashed these fears realizing that I had been keeping house since primary school. I applied and knew the battle was half won when I got the call for an interview.

The CFO's wife Gwen asked me the obvious interview questions, "Why do you want to be a housekeeper?" She was apprehensive but felt that I could perform the responsibilities with a minimal amount of guidance. Visions of my hands in the soapsuds by day and my nose blissfully in my texts at night were already dancing in my head.

Gwen presented me with a list of daily, weekly, and general responsibilities to peruse. Ironing, vacuuming, and laundry topped the list. "Can you do it?" she asked. *Nothing new*, I thought to myself. I've been ironing pillowcases since I was eight. *Vacuuming?* My house had a few nicked doorways, but no structural damage ever came from pulling mom's Electrolux around. *Washing clothes?* This duty necessitated separating the whites from the darks and keeping the reds separate from everything else. I knew that I could do the job.

I readily accepted when Gwen offered me the position.

My first day brought the fears any new job would bring—with a few extras. *You're no kid, Evelyn*, I said to myself. *You should be moving ahead rather than backwards*, but I was really looking forward to the change in pace. How often could I use my muscle instead of my mind—and make money?

Day One started off well. The CFO's wife treated me as a professional. "I am very particular and like everything done just so," she asserted.

Every day became an exercise in learning Gwen's particular way of doing things. I found myself thinking about procedures I had been performing for years.

Days crawled into weeks, and those plastic bags still would not fit snugly into the trash bins. Pleated, one-hundred percent cotton tuxedo shirts replaced the pillowcases of my youth.

Then there was the cooking.

The spaghetti I prepared at home never stuck together, but it chose May 25th, 1990, to start. The carrots turned black that same night. *What the heck is going on?* I asked myself. My black and white frock was slowly melting into gray—the newest color of my complexion.

As my tenure continued, my brain started playing tricks on me. Valuable sculptures peeled as I dusted them. Feet turned into miles as I ran back and forth along the ever growing one-hundred-fifty-foot hallway. The kitchen table mysteriously took on stains. I knew the next thing to happen would be my required attendance at a party with the Mad Hatter.

I told myself to give it more time.

One morning the CFO's wife insisted, "It turns out we really need a workhorse," as she turned to pick up the shrilly whistling kettle. "It's a simple case of not thinking the requirements through before I hired you."

I tried to see the humor in the situation, as this job was an experiment. My forte was people, not polishing.

I sighed as I gazed back into the mirror. My days as a housekeeper were over, but how could I waste my investment in the dress? It could double as a waitress's uniform! Off I skipped, tossing the frock into the laundry, and then thumbing my way through the classifieds. I was going to get my mileage out of that little black dress if it was the last thing I did. •

Copyright 2024, Evelyn Eickmeyer-Quiñones

Evelyn Eickmeyer-Quiñones is a caregiver, wife, writer, poet, photographer, and former educator. Her writings can be found in *Newsday*, *The Petigru Review*, and *Next Avenue*. Her award-winning photographs have been published in the *Kakalak Poetry Anthology* and *Moonshine Review*.

# Gladys—Rolling Down the Highway
## by Jeanne VanBuren

Gladys, the red 1971 Toyota station wagon, was crammed all the way with just a sliver of visibility for the rear-view mirror. With Genesis on the radio choreographing my cruising over the winding pass between Nevada and California, there was a loud bang with scraping metal sound interrupting my vehicle's dance at the crest.

This was the maiden solo road trip in this car. My graduation present, blue vinyl suitcases, were jammed with my cutoff shorts, my t-shirts, handmade sundresses and blouses, sandals and grocery store tennis shoes. My worldly possessions of a JC Penny sewing machine, comforter, and flat pillows were bundled for my escape from Pittsburgh, "P.A." to Santa Cruz, "C.A." in September 1977. I'd purchased Gladys with money saved during high school while working at the local ice cream store, Twin Kiss, and the dry cleaners.

Highway 80 is almost a straight-line of 2650 miles, through nine states-Pennsylvania, Ohio, Indiana, Illinois, Iowa, Nebraska Wyoming, Utah, Nevada, California. The adventure was "old school" with folded maps, USA Atlas, no GPS, no cell phones, no ATMs, credit card, nor CB radio. I had the front seat stuffed with bedding for sleeping in rest stops at the end of 700-mile-ish days. I was equipped with AM-only radio and only cash, but Gladys was also loaded with the ambitious dreams of a righteous teenager.

I played leapfrog with truckers, and along the way joined a few characters for lunch and conversations. Most truckers were veterans that had rambling stories if someone took the time to listen. AM radio signals don't carry the music very far so when not listening to the farm equipment commercials, I was singing songs from memory like "Itsy Bitsy Spider," and "Jingle Bells" to pass the time.

I packed typical unhealthy road trip snacks like Twizzlers, Cheez-its, chips and pop. I took breaks about every two hours for meals, gas, or bathroom breaks. The impetus for this trip was my family situation. I come from a crowd of 12 siblings with a dad who decided to charge me rent to live under his roof—his rules because I wasn't going to college after high school. I was now going somewhere; out of there, for sure, to a place I was wanted and could make my own rules.

Why California? Well, that is another story that involves driving the AL-CAN highway in July with my brother Bill who was transferred from infantry in Anchorage to officer training at West Point including 5100 miles of learning to drive a stick shift, observing the wildlife like moose, or grizzlies and picking up hitchhikers before the Canadian border! One of the hitchhikers, a drifter named Brad smelled like an oil pan and left our company in Banff. The other, a backpacker named Mark, who survived a canoeing disaster, was hitching a ride back to Santa Cruz. Mark departed to the right in Cheyenne on Highway 80 and we, Bill and I, took the left back to Pittsburgh. After chatting for a scandalous number of summer months, the Gladys adventure hatched all because of those paths crossed in Alaska with my late first husband.

By the time I determined what all that metal-scraping racket was through that sliver of visibility, I realized my spare tire had broken loose from the clamp holding it underneath Gladys. I eventually pulled over at the bottom of the hill about a mile down from that escaped tire. I trekked up the roadway to retrieve the runaway tire. Lucky for me, a ditch ran beside the road the same width as my spare. I was so proud of the coincidence that I wouldn't have to lug that heaviness a mile down the road. I put the tire in the ditch and walked alongside it.

I must have forgotten that gravity is a thing. I discovered I couldn't keep up with a tire rolling down a hill with just my hand on it. The tire picked up speed. Faster and faster, it accelerated. It bolted across two lanes of the west-bound highway. It hopped over the grassy median strip. It bounced over two lanes of east-bound traffic and leaped over cars. I guess it was fortunate the trip was "old school" because with cell-phone cameras, the scene today would have gone viral of this teenager chasing a rolling and bouncing tire down a mountain.

That tire managed not to hit anyone or anything and landed miraculously across from Gladys, four lanes over. I carried the tire, crossing the two east-bound lanes, the median strip and the two west-bound lanes then fastened the tire back up into its rightful place under the car.

*Gladys—Rolling Down the Highway*

Just as I was done stowing the spare into the clamp, a highway patrolman arrived, parked behind Gladys and got out to ask if I needed any assistance. Of all the thoughts that ran through my head, I simply chuckled, "Not anymore!" •

Copyright 2024, Jeanne VanBuren

Jeanne VanBuren lives in Winston Salem, North Carolina--by way of Chesapeake, Pittsburgh, Santa Cruz, and Austin—where she is a local crafter and storyteller. As a member of North Carolina Writers Network, this story is a spark towards more memories being written and edited as "Boy Mom of Five," "Dating Escapades" over 38 years, and "Growing up in a Crowd" of 12 siblings. Her annual Christmas writings, enjoyed by friends and family over 20 years, might just include the news of an action screenplay for her celebrity crush Jason Statham. She says we all have a story in us, get it out there!

# Risky Decisions
## by Susan W. Harris

At 10:30 p.m. on a chilly, moonless night, I entered the parking garage. I unlocked my car, an old red Audi that had given me nothing but grief since I bought it. *Behave*, I thought as I started the engine to head home.

Tonight, Syracuse University had a basketball game, and the crowds would be letting out about now. I was sure the main highway would be congested so I decided to take the short cut. Normally I avoided this route at night since it was desolate through forests and fields. My headlights were the only illumination as no other cars were on this lonely, divided four-lane road.

It was almost Thanksgiving 1987, and I had just attended a concert by the Syracuse Symphony, where I worked as Director of Development. As I drove, my thoughts basked in the afterglow of a successful evening, when I felt a slight jerk in the car. Immediately alert, I tensed, but after a few seconds it stopped. Then the car jerked more and started to slow down. Then I remembered I had been low on gas coming to work this morning. I had meant to stop at a gas station on the way home. I looked at my gauge—*empty*. Now the car only coasted, so I pulled onto the shoulder of the road. The car stopped; my heart pounded.

"IDIOT!" I shouted out loud.

*Okay, now what? I am a woman alone in a car on a lonely highway. No stores or houses for miles. Why did I decide to take this short cut? Foolish!*

*There is a trailer park down the road— a few miles. Do I walk there? The weather has turned cold, and I only have on a cocktail dress and high heels. My raincoat is lightweight. If I do reach the trailer park, who and what will I find there?*

*Or should I put on my emergency lights and tie a white rag to my door handle? But I just read about a woman being kidnapped two weeks ago in the city. The Syracuse police warned of a serial killer.*

*If only my husband hadn't missed his flight and had attended the concert with me. He isn't even home to wonder why I am so late.*

Of the two risky alternatives, I decided to wait in the car for someone to stop, and I prayed. After fifteen minutes, I only saw two other cars going the opposite way. I was feeling increasingly desperate.

Then headlights appeared in my rear-view mirror. They became brighter and a white pickup truck slowed down. The driver glanced sideways at me as the truck rolled past. It pulled onto the shoulder ahead of me and stopped.

*Now what do I do? I'm scared. What if the driver is a serial killer?*

A young man, mid-30s, got out and walked toward my car.

I opened my door and stood beside it. "Stop," I cried out. "Stay where you are."

"What seems to be the trouble Ma'am?" he asked.

"I'm out of gas," I said, then quickly asked, "What's your name, and why are you here on this lonely highway?"

"My name is Jim Thompson, and I am on my way home after work," he responded to my interrogation.

"Why are you working so late?" I persisted.

"I'm a nurse at Community General and worked the late shift."

*My God*, I thought, *that's my husband's hospital.* "*What's the name of the hospital's president?*" I continued, trying to sound brave.

"I don't know, Ma'am; I don't have much contact with the president," he said with a slight smile.

I thought, *He doesn't look like a serial killer*—whatever a serial killer looks like. *What do I do? Should I walk to the trailer park or ask for a ride?* Both were risky, but I decided.

"Can you give me a ride to my home in Manlius?"

"Yes, Ma'am. It's on my way home. I stopped because I thought you looked like you needed help."

Locking my car, I grabbed my purse and said another silent prayer, as I climbed into his truck. We started talking, and

*Risky Decisions*

he explained that he was subbing for a sick nurse on the night shift. This was not his usual night. He also said he was a new father. I noticed a picture of a baby pasted to his dashboard. I relaxed my body slightly but kept my hand on the inside door handle.

True to his word, he delivered me to my driveway. I thanked him profusely and tried to give him the $40 dollars in my wallet, but he refused. I dropped it on the car seat anyway, thinking, *What new parent doesn't need $40.*

Grateful that the world has good people like Jim in it, but shaking with relief, I opened my front door.

Thanksgiving indeed. •

Copyright 2024, Susan W. Harris

Susan W. Harris lives in Hilton Head, South Carolina, where she is a member of the Island Writers Network, (IWN). Her mother, a writer, encouraged her to write. Professionally she wrote grants and proposals for nonprofits. Poems and stories were published in the IWN anthology's recent two books. Currently, she is writing a novel inspired by the life of her grandmother and mother.

# God Winked
## by John Rumbold

Staring at the screen I thought, *This is folly! Why am I doing this? Taking five days out of my busy life, spending $750? I must be crazy thinking I should do this.*

The "Purchase Ticket" button was pulsing at me from the screen. What made me think I could write a book? Sure, I had written many technical papers during my career as an engineer. I had even presented these papers at conferences. But what made me think I could write prose?

The thought of taking a community college creative writing class at the age of 68 was terrifying—all those youngins staring at me day after day. And yet here I was, thinking of embarking on my first research journey before I had any inkling of how I could turn that experience into writing a prose piece about it. I was taking the train from Los Angeles to New York as Adelaide, the protagonist (and my mother) had done unaccompanied at the age of 13 in early March 1929.

It had been 18 years since she told me the secret of her years spent in Sumatra and Malaya. She was gone now, and I had the audacity to think now was the proper time, or the time at all, to write a book about it without any knowledge or experience in that art, that craft. Nevertheless, I clicked on the button. By 1929 the Atchison, Topeka and Santa Fe Railway's California Limited had been surpassed in luxury and speed by the Southwest Chief. But frugality required that young Adelaide would take the California Limited, Train #4 departing La Grande Station in Los Angeles at 6:15 pm. And depart she did on February 27, 1929, to escape the deprivation and abuse of her Great Aunt. Eighty-four years later I was booking the Amtrak Southwest Chief, Train #4 departing Union Station in Los Angeles at 6:15.

The Moorish-inspired La Grande Station, having suffered heavy damage in the 1933 Long Beach earthquake, ended passenger service when Union Station was opened in 1939 and was demolished in 1946. I would have to be satisfied with Union Station for this reenactment without coal fired steam.

Upon boarding, the steward showed me to my roomette whereupon I took out my notebook to begin recording my experiences. As we rolled through the desolate neighborhoods of Los Angeles, the steward walked by and handed me a ticket with the letter "F" on it. "This is your dining car ticket," he said. "When you hear this letter called over the public address go back to the dining car and wait for the waiter to seat you at the next available seat."

I arrived as instructed and was directed to a table for four with a mature couple sitting facing each other. I began a conversation with the woman across from me. It began with the usual small talk—where do you live, why are you taking this journey with all of the necessary follow-up questions.

Then I asked the woman, "What do you do?"

"I just recently retired," she said.,

"What did you do before you retired?"

"I had my own psychology practice for many years. It was a very busy practice and I decided it was time to retire about a year ago. I was very active with the American Psychological Association where I presented many papers on various topics that I had researched."

I thought how interesting. Similar to my career in scientific endeavors.

"And what are you doing now that you are retired?" I asked, always curious about how this retirement thing plays out.

"I'm writing poetry and prose," she answered matter of factly.

I was taken aback, dumbstruck. I pondered the thought that out of pure chance I was facing a person who made the same transition that I had agonized over for several months. As the silence approached palpable, I managed to gather my thoughts.

Without revealing my current anxieties over doing the same, I asked, "How did you make that transition from technical writing to writing prose?"

"I found this man in Beverly Hills who teaches something called Method Writing," she said. "It's sort of like method acting but for writing. I took many of his courses and they have been a tremendous help in my transition to becoming a writer."

I never knew about the God Wink theory before, but I have since found many writings on the subject. The idea that a divine source sometimes puts people or events in our path to encourage us or answer our trepidations when that source believes in our course or a different one was a source of reassurance. And now ten years later I have taken many Method Writing courses and never once have I stepped foot in a community college classroom. •

Copyright 2024, John Rumbold

During his career as an industrial engineer, John Rumbold, wrote several technical papers for presentation at conferences. Since retiring, he has spent ten years working on a creative non-fiction account of his mother's experiences during the 1930s living on a rubber plantation in Sumatra, a story she only shared with him in his adulthood. John studied writing in Los Angeles, where he lived, with noted writing teachers and published pieces through Orange County Writers (Calif.). John now lives in Mooresville, North Carolina, and is a member of the North Carolina Writers Network.

# How Bad Could It Be?
## by Phyliss Grady Adcock

I married my high school sweetheart and never even dated anyone else. After ten years of marriage, I found myself single and unprepared for the journey ahead. Everyone wanted to get me a blind date so I could get out there and see what I had missed. Okay. How bad could it be? I would soon suspect that my friends really did not like me.

My first blind date was a friend's boss, and I was very optimistic. He was a gentleman, intelligent, funny, and was willing to pay for my babysitter! We dated for three months, and I thought I had won the dating lottery. I should have wondered why this 35- year- old man had never been married. He was scared to death of commitment and when things were really going well, he disappeared. Back then women did not call to find out why. My confidence took a nosedive.

Number two was sent by a fellow teacher. I still can't forgive her for this winner. When the knock came at the door, I peeped through the door and was very pleased to see a Burt Reynolds look-a-like. Opening the door, I found a man dressed from head to toe in all black with a bright red tie. He looked just like he stepped off the Broadway stage of *Guys and Dolls*. We got into his yellow Corvette and left my parking lot going

60 miles an hour. That was the slowest speed of the night. He had planned a night at a local club for dancing. After two quick drinks he turned into one of my fifth-grade students. He began playing drums on the top of our table and cheering on the band as if we were at a ballgame. After one dance, I was ready for this nightmare to end. I told him my babysitter had to be home by 11. He didn't even remember that there was no child at my apartment, much less a babysitter. After some protesting, he agreed to take me home after some breakfast at IHOP. *How bad could that be?*

You can't imagine! When the waitress delivered the syrup-stained menus, he began to lick his. (*No, I did not make this up.*) I refused to order but had to watch him devour a sticky plate using his mouth, fingers, and an occasional lick of his wrists. The last memory I have is of a ridiculous man with puckered lips standing at my door as I slammed it in his face.

My prior date should have been a big enough red flag to stop me. However, this one I brought on myself. I asked the office manager of my apartment complex if I could use the clubhouse to teach aerobics. She told me I was in luck because the owner was in his office. I entered and found a man about 20 years my senior looking over blueprints. After explaining my request, he said he would love for me to use the clubhouse for free if I would go out to dinner with him that night. Once again, I asked myself, *How bad could it be?*

He arrived on time. That was the best part of the evening. He was dressed in a white double-breasted blazer with short sleeves. I didn't even know those existed. His gray chest hair was sufficient for a shirt, I guess. This was a long time ago, but his bell-bottom pants were definitely out. At the end of the bell-bottoms were white patent leather shoes with no socks. *Yes, I am a fashion snob, but really!*

Despite his sartorial senselessness, this man was a millionaire. He asked which restaurant I would like to visit. He reminded me that he owned all three. In self-defense, I asked which one was the darkest. I did survive the evening and got the clubhouse free, but I did not accept another dinner!

Alas, I am a slow learner. Along with these three, I would endure 41 more blind dates. *How bad could it be?* Out of the 44, only five were normal. Not great, but normal. Then the 45th date would be "The Keeper"!

All I can say is that the dating pool, like the deep dark ocean is often filled with unbelievable creatures. It takes a lot of courage to dive in and continue to tread water. And it's true what the modern fairy tale tells us American women these days: "Before you find that handsome prince, you have to kiss a lot of toads." •

Copyright 2024, Phyliss Grady Adcock

After teaching 34 years, Phyliss Grady Adcock retired in Morehead City, North Carolina. She was recognized as the first Raychem Educator of the Year and is listed in Who's Who Among America's Teachers for 1996 and 2000. Her writing has appeared in *Mailbox Magazine*, *Teacher's Helper*, and five previous PSPP anthologies. Beginning 13 years ago, she created Senior Stretch, a program for Senior Citizens to promote healthy movement and social interaction.

She teaches life skills and creative writing for the Peer Recovery Center. Writing is her Happy Place.

# Band of Brothers
## by Janice Luckey

You have heard the adage "boys will be boys." It seems, well, incomprehensible as I dip my pizza crust into tangy olive oil and look at the three distinguished gentlemen sitting across from me in the pizza restaurant. Could they have once been scamps? Every few months my husband gathers with his older and younger brothers to catch up on current news and inevitably to retell the stories of their childhood. With parents and sister long gone, this ritual is important—to nail down a shared past. After all, only these three will remember the stories, even if they don't agree on the details sometimes. "No, Mrs. Christianson was my second-grade teacher, not third. I remember because I loved her." Over sweet tea and Diet Coke, the three devoted brothers tighten the strands of their DNA into a bond so strong it will survive long after they have passed from this troubled planet.

I have known these three balding, arthritic guys for 50 years. It is hard to imagine them making foolish choices. But …

The youngest brother at the age of 18 bought a gold 650cc Kawasaki and a monkey. He named the monkey Banana. Banana liked to bite people on the neck. When he regained his senses, he got rid of the motorcycle and the monkey. Then, he up and joined the Navy and just as rashly married the wrong girl. "Dumb," he says, "everything I did was dumb, but I don't want the whole world to know." Therefore, he shall remain anonymous, and we can only wonder what he is not saying. He did in time find the right girl and they have been married for over 40 years, and he's never owned another monkey. He also takes pride in the service he gave to his country. As we say in the South, he smartened up.

My husband has always looked up to his older brother, but one day Michael would be at my husband's mercy. In the 1960's, Charlotte's I-85 was not the current clog of cars it is today. That stretch of highway did teem with fast moving cars and trucks. Certainly, no place for pedestrians! The two brothers, though, ran across it each day to and from school. One day after school Michael and a friend were chasing each other through the woods adjacent to school when Michael ran at full speed into a tree. The blow knocked him to the ground and upon rising the boys discovered Michael could not see. My husband insisted they go back to school for help, but Michael was adamant to go home. So, my husband, Steve, led his blind brother toward home, but how would they cross the traffic on the interstate in that condition? With Michael holding Steve's shirt tail, Steve strategized to get them halfway across the highway to the grassy median. Next, he waited with trembling hands for just the right moment to navigate them over the other half of the road. Succeeding at that by the grace of God, they started their 30-minute walk home. After a trip to the hospital emergency room, doctors declared Michael fine and the blindness only temporary. The dangerous dash across the interstate was not one of the boys' best decisions, giving personal meaning to the phrase "blind faith."

Keeping the family narratives going, my husband tells of the winter of 1961 when Charlotte experienced three consecutive Wednesday snowstorms. With school closed, the boys in the neighborhood slipped and slid around an old-abandoned racetrack at the bottom of the hill. In the summer, the racetrack surrounded a pond overrun by reeds and cattails, however, from the snow storms the pond now looked to be solid ice. What possessed my husband—the middle child—to walk to the center of the pond, I have no idea. But he did, and fell through the thin ice, sinking immediately up to his waist in red mud. As the sucking mud pulled him down, he yelled for help. His best friend, Marty, came to the rescue and tugged Steve out of the mire, covering himself in mud as well. After the harrowing experience and freezing cold they arrived home only to be in trouble with their mothers for being muddy! Steve lost a boot in the pond which his mom seemed maddest about. With her three, she was probably accepting that "boys will be boys" but I am pretty sure she was sternly pronouncing, "Do NOT bring that mud IN. TO. THIS. HOUSE!"

---

After coffee and cannoli and fleeting hours reminiscing in the restaurant, we part, always promising to get together again soon. It is a commitment no one takes lightly. In our waning years, it is the stories that bind us together—the good, the bad, the ugly. And most gratefully, the foolhardiness we have all survived. •

*Band of Brothers*

Copyright 2024, Janice Luckey

Janice Luckey, who lives in Mooresville, North Carolina, remembers when writing became a rhythm of her life. She scribbled a romance novel in a 3-ring binder in junior high school sparking a life-long love of all things writerly—writing, reading, journaling and hoarding office supplies. Janice is fueled by the love and support of her family and most anything chocolate. When not writing, she can be found making memories with her husband and four granddaughters, or roaming the aisles at the library, bookstores, and Staples.

# The Empire of Death
## by Erika Hoffman

When young, everyone does foolish things, especially young males. Also, youthful gals do stupid stuff like hitchhiking in Europe, or scuba diving after one short class in a pool in St. Thomas, or maybe imbibing some concoction at a frat party from a large container, which is full of grain alcohol. Yeah. Nowadays, psychological studies show that good judgment or medium prudence or lack of reckless behavior doesn't take hold until after one passes the mid-20s. Blame it on biology!

Nonetheless, sometimes, an older version of a former foolish risk taker does something that may defy good common sense. Once in a blue moon, a body engages in an activity that is at odds with the maternal body you presently inhabit. As a female matures, she defines adventure differently.

Around Halloween, 2023, my husband and I travelled to Paris with friends about our age. They wanted to take the hop-on hop-off bus and lunch at the Eiffel Tower. Ho-hum. Not "*moi.*" I planned to visit a network of tunnels with a macabre history and an entrance sign that reads: "*Arrete! C'est ici L'empire de la Mort!*"

I had researched the Catacombs. You could buy tickets a week

ahead of time but not earlier than that. When purchasing them, I read the warnings on the site: 243 steep stairs, in toto: 131 steps down to the burial pits and 112 up to the exit.
No one with respiratory issues should go, nor should anyone with physical disabilities. There are no lavatories in the caves. The winding tunnels cannot accommodate folks walking side-by-side. Folks with claustrophobia ought not enter. Sensitive individuals are discouraged. Folks with heart conditions are warned to stay away. Tourists with agility issues better not try. Drips from the limestone overhead form huge puddles on the floor. The lights could go out. You might trip; there are stumbling stones. It's forbidden to touch any bones or skulls lining the walls to balance you. It's not advised to take children under the age of 14. There's no place to buy food or drink. In certain spots, the ceiling has caved in—sink holes. There are off-limits areas and tunnels: Don't go there. It's a self-guided tour. It would be impossible to carry a stretcher down. The walkways can be slippery. It's gruesome and ghoulish. Although 150 miles of tunnels exist, only one mile is open to tourists.

I wanted to see it.

"What if I turn my ankle?" I asked my husband.

"I'm not carrying you up 112 spiral stone steps."

"If I have a panic attack?"

"Carry a paper bag with you?"

"What if anxiety causes my A-fib to act up?"

"This is your idea, you know. I don't mind re-visiting the Eiffel Tower."

"Everyone visits that iron structure, which I've done. You've done. Exploring these ancient quarries turned into ossuaries will be memorable."

Who knew this underground network had been mined by the Romans and that this catacomb of artfully organized skulls and femurs had been added after 1774 to solve two problems? There were mine cave-ins. The limestone for such architectural marvels, as the Louvre and Notre-Dame, came from under the city; occasionally, sink holes developed and houses tumbled into these quarries. In addition, the city's graveyards were overcrowded with unsanitary conditions. Therefore, in 1786, this ossuary was consecrated after the contents of the city's graves were dumped into these pits. Six million souls' bodies inhabit the catacombs, including famous ones like Moliere, Robespierre, and the sisters of French kings.

"Byron, you think I can walk the height of a five-story building?"

My silent husband raised his eyebrows.

"I won't take my pocketbook. We'll need a jacket, though. It's only 57 degrees."

I'm not gonna lie and say the journey down the spiral stairs and along the skull-strewn narrow passages isn't unnerving. I kept a mantra going in my head that this was like a fun house at Halloween, and that there is an end to it all. I took photos, but it seemed unseemly asking my husband to pose in front

*The Empire of Death*

of a macabre skull which once had been a real head on a live person. An American family behind us on the corridor had an annoying 11-year-old who'd sob sporadically, "Mama, I don't want to die down here." I also noticed no one as old as we two were exploring the underground sepulcher.

When we finally emerged and headed for the metro station at Denfert-Rochereau, I said gleefully, "Folks at home warned about pickpockets and bedbugs on the subway. Little do those folks know about our nerves of steel!"

As I was congratulating our intrepidness, a velo swerved dangerously close to my husband who had stepped off the curb. "Attention!" the cyclist yelled to my brave explorer husband.

"Close call, Columbus," I whispered. •

Copyright 2024, Erika Hoffman

Erika Hoffman is a happy and longtime resident of beautiful North Carolina. She's a member of three writing clans: North Carolina Writers Network; The Triangle Area Freelancers; and Carteret Writers. During the past 14 years while pursuing "her scrivener dream," she has succeeded in getting published 460 times. Yet, Erika deems her best achievement— besides being married forever—is having raised four functioning citizens. Without a doubt, her proudest moniker is "Ama' to six grandsons and three grand-daughters.

## Our Little Bit of Heaven
### by Janet K. Baxter

We needed land, preferably with a house, but definitely land enough for a small barn and pasture. The barn where I boarded my two mares was no longer available and I needed to move them quickly. My husband found a house with seven acres just a short drive from the park where I often rode. We drove out to view the property, walk the acreage, and look in the windows of the vacant house. The location and land were doable. I barely looked at the house.

The next day, after one walk-through and another look over the property we decided to buy. Before moving, I pored over "farming on small acreage" books to design a barn, a dry lot, a small paddock behind one stall, and two acres for pasture. My laser focus was solely on the horses and their needs. Fencing was installed and a 4-horse barn was built. I rarely thought of the house. Just before Christmas that year, we moved the horses, the dogs and cats, our youngest son, and the contents of our home to the new property.

Soon after closing, we began to see issues that we had not counted on. The previous owner had hedged on the efficiency of the water-based heat pump. He failed to mention that it broke down frequently with only one person in the county who could coax it back to life. The first time it failed for us was on a Sunday during that first January when the temperature fell to a bone-chilling 15 degrees. Even with a roaring fire in the fireplace, the living room remained below 60. Travis arrived Monday morning, regaling about the times the system had failed and which components had already been replaced. It took another two days for parts to arrive. Travis became part of the family as the system repeatedly failed when temperatures went below freezing or above 95 degrees.

The 1970's house had shabby gold and avocado green carpet and dated avocado green appliances. An easy fix we thought. Over time, we remodeled each room. However, with each project, we discovered what we had missed in that quick, one-visit walk-through. We found that the outside walls were made with concrete block and the inside walls were built with metal studs. The front door was a thick metal door with 2x4 boards glued on that were then painted battleship gray; the mantel above the fireplace was made of 2x6 boards. The floors in each room had to be rebuilt to lay new wood or tile floors. Each remodeling project was an engineering and financial nightmare.

Due to the iron in the rock, our little mountain ridge draws lightning which frequently takes out the invisible fencing system, the well-pump, and the internet system. One strike landed so close to the house that garden rocks in the back yard were blown over the house landing in my rose garden. The barn is equally at risk. With each rainfall, the "dry" lot next to the barn turns into a 6-inch-deep mud lot. One spring, a wind shear caused the barn roof to set sail and land in the ravine. During a freeze, the barn stalls flooded caused by cracked water pipes under the concrete hall; another year the pipes froze under the house. A tornado caused roof damage to the house and barn with its large hail and strong winds.

My husband is on a first-name basis with all the repair men for the barn, the well, plumbing, electricity, invisible fencing, tree service, and roofers.

Although these challenges were frustrating and inconvenient, recalling each now makes us laugh and marvel at our persistence and ingenuity. Over the years, the remodeled house has become ours. We've added eight acres of land. We've planted two hybrid elm and two hybrid chestnut trees in hopes of seeding the forest that grows to our south. We've planted raspberry bushes in front of the barn and blueberry bushes around the yard which provide ready snacks spring and summer. Our small orchard now has apple, pear, cherry, and peach trees. Around the house, we've planted native plants for the butterflies, hummingbirds, song birds, and insects. Bluebird nesting boxes dot our property. Two nesting boxes by the barn have successful nests each year.

Our yard sings each spring, summer, and fall with local and migrating birds. Just recently, we made the sunroom into my writing and thread painting studio with bird feeders located outside the windows. I now enjoy bird escapades at the feeders and watch my three horses, Melody, Nugget, and Cappy, in the pasture while I work. We have our little bit of heaven. •

*Our Little Bit of Heaven*

Copyright 2024, Janet K. Baxter

Janet K. Baxter lives in Kings Mountain, North Carolina, and is a member of Scribblers, a memoir critique group. Her stories, "Horse Whispering for the Average Woman," "Southern Blues," "A Frank Lesson," "Cappie, The Boomerang Horse," "An Angel's Smile," "Morgan: Our Escape Artist," "One Soul Alone," "Forest Bathing on Horseback," and "Horsehair in the Hummingbird Nest" appeared in previous anthologies published by the Personal Story Publishing Project. Retired, Janet enjoys thread painting, trail riding, writing, and all the delights of her "mini-estate": www.mountaingaitacres.com.

# Double Trouble
## by Barbara Houston

Despite their antics which began at an early age, my twin brothers survived childhood. A miracle.

Our young family lived in a second story apartment in West Virginia. One sweltering day, Mother briefly left the living room where the boys were playing. John and Jim (not yet 2) pushed the screen out of the open window. One was on the roof, and the other had one leg out the window just as Mother entered the room. She pulled one twin back inside and crawled onto the roof to rescue the other.

As they grew older, Jim, who was accident prone, emerged as the ringleader. My brothers enjoyed playing cowboys and Indians with friends. They whittled the tips of their handmade arrows down to sharp points and shot them at each other with bows. An arrow hit Jim's nose bone and went into the fleshy part of his face. If it had been one-eighth inch closer, he would have lost his left eye.

Jim had another accident while riding his bike. Trying to impress two girls, he stood up on the bicycle seat. The bike hit a rock and sent him flying over the handlebars. This resulted in a hospital visit and a concussion.

*Double Trouble*

"Yeah, I really impressed them," Jim said.

Another close call followed. Anxious to try out a bicycle that a neighbor gave them, John sat on the seat and Jim sat on the handlebars facing forward. As they coasted down a steep hill toward a busy intersection, they realized that the brakes did not work. They picked up speed and flew across Main Street, screaming frantically and narrowly avoiding heavy cross traffic.

Escapades continued as they got older. Walking home with high school friends, they decided to take a shortcut across a railroad bridge which stood high above the Kanawha River.

"It's fine," one said. "No trains coming."

Nearing the end of the bridge, they heard the train whistling behind them. Sprinting the rest of the way, they barely reached the other side as the train rushed by.

My brothers slept in a converted basement room. With no outside door, they would occasionally crawl out of their bedroom window during the night to meet some of their buddies and walk to the other side of town, not the safest place to be. One evening, the boys passed a building where a lively group of young men and women was partying.

Thinking he was being funny, Jim yelled something as a taunt.

A group of the revelers ran down the stairs and chased them until they escaped. On another excursion across town, the friends spotted a red light in front of a building, a house of prostitution. These hormonal teenage boys enjoyed watching the activities at the house as half-naked women leaned out the windows. One of the boys yelled something idiotic which provoked a chase from some of the male clients. The boys got away again, but would they NEVER learn?

Dad loaned Jim the car one night. After picking up his friend and the friend's girlfriend, they headed to a party. The girl's mother gave them an 11:00 P.M. curfew. Late leaving the party, Jim sped home on narrow winding roads and made it to the girl's house just one minute late. The twins sometimes "borrowed" the car after our parents went to bed. We lived on a hill, so the driver would release the emergency brake, let the car coast to the bottom of the hill, then turn on the ignition. Before returning, they put gas in the car and parked it in the same spot on the street.

John and Jim attended Stonewall Jackson High School in Charleston. South Charleston High School was their biggest rival. Friday evening before a big game, Jim, John, and a car full of friends went to a pep rally at South Charleston. Jim wore his Stonewall Jackson jacket. *What could possibly go wrong?* After some taunting from their rivals, a student punched John in the face. Their friends pulled Jim away after he tackled the boy. They sprinted to Hershel's car, jumped in, and sped off just as a brick flew through the window, grazing Hershel's shoulder and covering everyone with shards of glass.

Hershel yelled, "I can't drive. I have glass in my eyes."

"Keep going," the others yelled. "They're chasing us."

*Double Trouble*

Once safely away, John drove Hershel to the hospital where the doctor removed several small pieces of glass from his eyes.

Surprisingly, our parents never found out about my brothers' teenage exploits. Surely guardian angels protected them from their foolish ventures. They survived to become mature, responsible adults. John is respected and active in his church. Jim became a cop—but he still likes to speed. •

Copyright 2024, Barbara Houston

Barbara Houston lives in Matthews, North Carolina. A member of Scribblers, a memoir writing group, she writes stories about her life and family to pass on to her children and grandson. "In Bear Country," "Music Box Memories," "Dark Water," and "Elephant Encounters" were published in previous anthologies through the Personal Stories Publishing Project. In addition to writing, Barbara enjoys reading fiction, singing with the Charlotte Singers, spending time with family and friends, and travelling with her husband, Jerry. She says, "Being retired is the best job I ever had."

# They Say It's Like Riding a Bike
## by Frances Rinaldi

One glorious Florida Sunday morning my husband, Andre handed me an article about a woman who rode her bike across the United States with a group raising money for breast cancer awareness. He felt the article would be of interest because my mother was a breast cancer survivor. What he could not have anticipated was how it would change my life—and his, it seems.

Working since age 15 and while raising a family, I had taken little time to be adventurous. I found myself jealous of this woman's freedom to take off and travel for months, spared of life's interruptions. When I mentioned my decision to ride a bike across the United States to my husband, his response increased my desire to do it. "Don't you think you should at least get a bike and ride it around the block once." Andre had played almost every sport in college and is a black belt in Judo. He had always been athletically inclined. I was not.

Two days later his brother asked if we could store his bicycle for a month while he was out-of-town. We'd be happy to, I said, as long as I could ride it. Step 1.

I knew better than to tell anyone of my decision to challenge myself. Critics will always tell you that you're either too old, or too young, or not smart enough, or too something. So, I asked a friend, a runner, if she would cycle with me. She said she'd be happy to ride with me if I ran with her. Step 2.

The stories of shame and humiliation that followed in participating in runs, marathons, and triathlons could fill pages. Early on, I entered a 5K. I was so slow a blind man and his dog passed me. I was second-to-last and still received a first-place trophy. I was first in my age division. I was the only one in my age division. But I endured the embarrassment while secretly staying motivated in my preparing to ride across the United States.

What I did not realize at the time was how I was changing. I was healthier. I was making new friends. I was taking on challenges, all for my one secret event.

Life has its challenges though. A month before leaving to ride across the United States, a cycling accident would keep my secret safe for another six months. In a triathlon, I hit a cone to avoid hitting another cyclist. My clipless pedals did not dislodge, and at 23 miles per hour I went up in the air and came down on my back. I suffered a cracked skull, a broken pelvis, ribs, and wrist. Six months later, I faced the challenge of getting over the fear of riding. I signed up for a ride with a group, Woman's Tours, cycling across the southern tier of the United States. Step 3.

Day 1presented one of the challenges that would surface all along this journey. I had never cycled up a hill like this before.

I'd thought we'd ease into higher elevations. Not so. Starting from San Diego, California, reaching our first stop would be an Alpine climb.

I pounded up the mountain. At the top I was so tired I could not unclip from my pedals, I let my bike fall over into a grassy field. That night I was too tired to eat, I had a splitting headache, and I was nauseated. I was sure I would be heading home on Day 2. However, good fortune came my way in the form of a wonderful woman. Donna was 76, I was 52. She took me under her wing saying she had been impressed at my performance, but that if I tried that again I would more than likely not finish a second day's ride. She was shocked I had decided to do this ride without having done at least a small ride in hill country. Yet graciously she took time to teach me how to shift gears and to manage hills on a bike.

She asked me why I had decided to do this ride. I said I wanted to do something unique before I was too old. She laughed, pointing out that she was old enough to be my mother. Old is a state of mind, after all, not a number. Thanks to Donna's support and influence, I, now at her age then, continue cycling. I've cycled crossed the United States in five different directions and in several countries.

Of course, without Andre's support none of that could have come to pass. To his credit, my initially skeptical husband has joined the world of cycling, too. Together we bike onward. And when life offers us either joys or troubles, one of us is often heard to offer, "Life—they say it's just like riding a bike." •

*They Say It's Like Riding a Bike*

Copyright 2024, Frances Rinaldi

Frances Rinaldi lives in Melbourne, Florida, where she has been sharing stories from history, about nature, and personal experiences in schools, organizations, and theater for thirty years. She belonged to Terra Sancta Press editing group and Brevard Theatrical Ensemble for over twenty years. She has published seven books. Two children's, one environmental, and one travel book under her name, and a collection of three suspense books under her pen name F.R. Merrill.

# Class V

by Jane Satchell McAllister

Standing at the base of the Summersville Dam in West Virginia and watching streams of water jet out from the three huge cylindrical pipes with enough force to remain suspended for over 20 feet before crashing into the Gauley riverbed, I felt my heart rate accelerate and wondered just what I was doing here.

Moving to Washington, D.C., after graduation, I quickly connected with several area volleyball leagues. My co-ed team enjoyed annual rafting trips on the Gauley River each fall when the Army Corps of Engineers released water from the dam over the course of six weeks. Rafting enthusiasts from around the country converged on the area to ride its multitude of Class V rapids (on a scale from I to VI). The roar of the water spewing out of the pipes drowned out any attempts at conversation, though my friends saw from the look on my face that I felt both terrified and exhilarated.

Rafting the Gauley is not a float trip. Our outfitter and his crew explained how to sit securely in the raft, paddle effectively, and, most importantly, to obey the shouted commands of the guide seated at the back of the raft. Such instructions were critical because the speed and force of the current as the river dropped and wound around boulders and whirlpools were sufficient to suck rafters out of the raft and even pin them under rocks. Lives are lost on the river.

That first time down the river hooked me. The thrill and challenge of charging down that churning river, paddling left and right to skirt dangers and eddies, dropping so fast that our butts bounced off of the sides, and finally safely arriving at the pullout point whetted my appetite for more. For most of the ensuing ten years, I reserved a fall trip on the Gauley, bringing various groups with me to share in the incredible experience.

Late in the spring semester of my first year of graduate school, my class was tasked with giving a persuasive presentation. I talked the class through an early morning trip down the Gauley River, ending with a call to action, signing up for a spring raft trip, which would be calmer than during the scheduled fall releases. Close to 30 crazy people enlisted, making me immensely popular with Frank, our preferred outfitter.

Frank served as our raft guide, and I sat beside him at the back, since he wanted to evaluate my potential as a river guide. My future husband, Charlie, joined us as well. As we steered into a tight series of Class V rapids known as Lost Paddle, I wedged myself on the back seat. A moment later, I surfaced in the water behind the raft with no actual memory of leaving the raft. Fortunately, Frank grabbed me and threw me back into the boat while still shouting commands to get us through the rapids. Charlie had no idea I had been swept out until after the trip. He never rafted with me again. Happily, all of us made it back to Charlottesville.

In September 1989, about 25 banking buddies were scheduled to join me for a Gauley raft trip. As it happens, Hurricane Hugo blew through the Carolinas and continued northward through Virginia and West Virginia just before our trip. A couple of folks backed out but the rest of us decided to proceed. Charlie's parents called us the day after the storm. Charlie's mom asked him to tell me not to go because it was too dangerous. I can still hear him saying, "Mom, I cannot tell her that," knowing that I would not be dissuaded. Off we went to experience Class V rapids after a Category 5 storm.

That river trip set a speed record with unprecedented water levels in the river. I recall at one point seeing in my peripheral vision a wave of water off to my right that was higher than my head. One of the party fell into the river, losing his glasses, and had to float through a rapid before his boat guide could haul him back in. He absolutely loved the experience and swore he would return. Others made clear that this was their first and last whitewater rafting trip. I could have wiped out a third of the corporate trust department, but fortunately we all made it back with bragging rights for days to follow.

Pushing the edge like I had done on the Gauley taught me to expand my comfort zone, paying dividends many times over in both my personal and professional life. Though the degree of risk and wildness has diminished with time, I still bask in an accelerated heartbeat brought on by embracing the extraordinary. •

*Class V*

Copyright 2024, Jane Satchell McAllister

Jane Satchell McAllister's writings draw inspiration from the wide variety of people and places she encounters, from her home base in Davie County, North Carolina, to rich adventures across our country and abroad. She has co-authored two Images of America books through Arcadia Publishing and served for nine years as director of the county public library. Her current writing project is compiling stories based on decades of travel, both fiction and nonfiction, almost as much fun as the trips themselves.

# Partners
## by Robin Gaiser

Katie called me to set up guitar lessons, playing and singing country music, her goal. At the appointed hour, a beige Mercedes coupe drove into my driveway. I waved from my front door then watched her slide out of her seat and stand: a tall, slender woman with long, long gray curly hair down her back. Her floral dress nearly touched her feet. In her 70s, I guessed.

She opened the trunk and lifted out a white, hard guitar case with "*GUILD*" emblazoned on the side. Already I was jealous.

"I got this guitar at auction. Any good?"

I could hardly speak. "You got a treasure."

"That's good. I paid $600 for it."

"A steal." She was pleased with my comment.

Katie could neither tune nor play that gorgeous Guild. And she couldn't carry a tune or keep time.

The next week and the next, she showed up carrying a satchel along with the Guild and her handbag. Sorghum molasses, potted daisies; rhubarb, green beans, tomatoes. Dandelion wine. She asked if I wanted a kitten or puppy. "I'm not lucky like you. I don't have kids. Rescues are my babies."

Katie arrived faithfully each week bearing gifts and a huge smile. I suspected she was lonely. She spoke disparagingly of her husband, Howard, a retired lawyer. "He's a drunk now. And mean."

Katie invited me and my husband to join her at a country music venue, Partners 2, out her way in then-rural Centreville, Virginia. "I'll go early and gets seats."

We found our way to the ramshackle building with a blinking neon Partners 2 sign. Before we left our car, we could hear bluegrass music. When Gordon opened the door into the club, a whoosh of cigarette smoke and sour beer odor hit us in the face. The place was packed.

Katie waved from a long table near the dance floor. Folks sized us up and down as we inched our way through the crowd. I sat down next to her, and Gordon wound his way to a seat across from us. A man in a black cowboy hat slapped him on the back. Gordon looked stunned. "That's Jack. Don't pay him no mind. He's just bein' friendly," Katie shouted across the table.

Like other women, Katie wore a low-cut frilly blouse and colorful ruffled skirt blown up with crinolines. The men were outfitted in Western shirts, cowboy boots and hats, and tight black slacks studded with rhinestones. No wonder we stood out in our preppy clothes. Couples two-stepped, flat-footed, waltzed, and dipped together on the dance floor while the band, a tight ensemble of five bluegrass musicians, effortlessly passed around solo breaks.

Beer sloshed, people conversed loudly enough to be heard above the band, and men threw their heads back and laughed heartily. Everyone knew each other. When the band took a break, recorded country music blasted in its place.

At one point I saw Kaite reach down into a fancy leather purse laid flat on her lap. Something shiny caught my eye as she slid it out of her handbag then pulled out a tissue. My breath caught: Katie was holding a pistol.

She must have registered my shock. "Oh, I never leave home without it. There's danger out there." Just like that she returned the pistol to her purse and resumed her focus on the band and dancers.

That gun next to me robbed my concentration. I finally leaned over to Katie's ear, thanked her and made up an excuse about our babysitter's curfew. Gordon saw me stand and motion my head toward the front door.

I kept silent until we got in our car. "Guess what Katie had in her purse?" I paused. "A pistol."

"No way," he said.

"Yep. She pulled it out to get some tissues. A little gun with a pink mother of pearl handle. The barrel was pointed right at my lap."

"I'm glad I wasn't sittin' next to her," he said. "If that thing fired, it could be the end of the family jewels."

I sighed out loud. But was glad for his sick humor.

After six months of weekly lessons, Katie decided she just wasn't able to play the guitar. "Let's stay in touch. Keep comin' out to Partners." We hugged long and hard. She packed up that Guild and said good-bye.

The last I heard from Katie was more *what I read* about her in *The Washington Post.* This dear sweet woman with the big heart had been arrested. A neighbor smelled strong odors emanating from Katie's property and called the police. The cops found more than fifty cats and dogs living in her barn. I was relieved the smell was just that and not "mean Howard's" mouldering body that drew such attention. •

Copyright 2024, Robin Gaiser

Robin Russell Gaiser holds degrees in English literature and psychology and a certificate in therapeutic music. An experienced multi-instrumentalist and vocalist, Robin gave guitar and dulcimer lessons and performed with The Mill Run Dulcimer Band while she lived in northern Virginia. Memories of students and Band fans offer rich ideas for stories, like "Partners." Robin is a published author of two memoirs: *Musical Morphine: Transforming Pain One Note at a Time* (Pisgah Press: 2016), and *Open for Lunch* (Pisgah Press; 2018). A third book is underway. She and her husband live in Asheville, North Carolina. www.robingaiser.com

# Up in the Air
## by S. G. Benson

Flying has always fascinated me. As a kindergartner walking home from school, I stretched out my arms and imitated birds cavorting overhead.

Our family took my grandmother to the San Diego airport to catch a flight in 1958. From the outdoor boarding gate, she climbed the wheeled stairs to the plane and waved to us from the top step. The propeller engines revved, and I covered my ears and laughed as the prop-wash hit us.

I often flew on commercial flights as I grew older. Arizona, with its crystal-clear skies, became my favorite destination. I moved to Flagstaff for college and those skies began calling me in earnest. I booked a ticket on a commercial "puddle jumper" from Flagstaff to Phoenix. The last one to board, I entered the cabin and looked around. A passenger occupied every seat. *Where do I go?*

The pilot sat alone in the cockpit. He beckoned, pointing to the empty copilot's seat beside him. I strapped myself in.

We cleared the treetops, and I pointed out the window to a forested subdivision. "There's my house!" The pilot dipped one wing and circled it. During the next half hour, he provided a running commentary on the scenery.

"Okay," he said, sitting up straighter in his seat. "We have to clean up our act before entering Phoenix air space."

We landed at Sky Harbor International. As we taxied to the gate, he winked at me and put his finger to his lips.

I looked into the cost of flying lessons. I couldn't afford it. The following year I saw an ad for a Quicksilver ultralight airplane. I *could* afford that, so I bought it. Gorgeous, it had bright orange Dacron wings stretched over an aluminum-tubed frame. It had a single seat, one propeller, and a tiny motor. It looked like a go-kart with wings and a parachute.

I found an instructor, Dan, who agreed to take payments. I trailered my ultralight to a little airstrip near Phoenix and felt disappointed when Dan told me to park it for six weeks while he taught me to fly in his two-seat trainer. "You'll be glad you did," he said.

Every Saturday I drove to the desert and learned to fly. After classroom instruction on the plane, weather, and laws, Dan fired up the trainer and I clambered into the second seat. We climbed to about 300 feet. He gave me the stick and I steered.

Landing became my biggest challenge. Dan modeled the patience of Job as he helped me, again and again, to make the right approach to touch down gently on the dirt strip. More often than not I'd misjudge our height and either come in too low and hit hard or come in too high and drop straight down the final three feet. Either way, it was tough on the plane and our tailbones.

At the end of week six, Dan asked, "Do you think you're ready to solo?"

I wheeled out my Quicksilver and conducted the pre-flight check under Dan's watchful eye. I cinched my helmet's chin strap tight and climbed into the seat. Dan gave me a thumbs-up, and I started down the runway, pulling back the stick slightly as I reached take-off speed. I climbed a few feet and then froze, unable to will my hand to guide me higher. I flew the entire length of the strip at an altitude of five feet. As the end of the runway neared, I glided into my very first perfect landing. Dan doubled over with laughter.

I pulled myself together and, with what was left of my dignity, tried again. This time I soared high, and two geese appeared out of nowhere, flying just off my wing tip. I had at last achieved my dream of soaring with the birds.

After that, I flew often. One day while I was in the air, a *real* airplane landed on the little runway. I remembered my training—Dan warned me not to follow too closely if that ever happened because an airplane leaves behind an invisible track of turbulence that can easily upset an ultralight.

After the Cessna landed, I circled the strip several times before making my approach. I did not wait long enough. I struck the turbulence about 30 feet above the ground and it flipped my craft 90 degrees. Still flying, but with one wing pointing at the sky and the other within 18 inches of the sunflower field that lined the airstrip, I saw my life pass quickly in front of my eyes.

I'm still not sure how I managed it but, somehow, I climbed back to a safe altitude. I circled for a long, long time, enjoying being up in the air before I worked up the nerve to land.

Learning to fly freed me to follow my dreams. It still gives me confidence and reinforces what I've always known about taking the time to learn and prepare. Dan is gone now, but his words still ring true: "You'll be glad you did." •

Copyright 2024, S. G. Benson

S. G. (Sandy) Benson lives in Warne, North Carolina, where she is a member of the North Carolina Writers Network-West. Her work has appeared in numerous magazines and newspapers, and she received awards from the Nebraska Press Women. She published her first book in 2021, *My Mother's Keeper: One Family's Journey Through Dementia*. Her second book, *Dear Folks: Letters Home from World War II, 1943-1946* was released in 2024. She is working on a manuscript collection of autobiographic short stories, "Girls Can't Do That." Details at https://www.sandygbenson.com/

# The General
by Peter Holsapple

My grandfather was a retired brigadier general in the United States Marine Corps.

He was a thick slab of a man who could freeze an entire restaurant mid-rush with a giant explosive sneeze. He sang "Abdul Abulbul Ameer" with gusto at the top of his lungs at the drop of a hat. He wrote sappy love lyrics to my grandmother, and he doted on his two daughters. And the Christmas after he died, there was my first electric guitar under the tree, his gift from beyond the grave.

His most notable accomplishment may have been that he had run for U.S. President on the Constitution Party's ticket in the state of Washington in the 1960 election; he also ran for Vice-President in Texas the same year, putting him into a uniquely weird corner of the country's political record books. The Constitution Party's platform made the John Birch Society look like a church picnic full of pantywaists, supporting isolationism and racial segregation.

Suffice to say, with opponents like John F. Kennedy and Richard Nixon, his miniscule vote totals did not make him a household name; the extremism and ugliness of his politics were and still are a source of embarrassment.

His family saw him as having been an easy mark by Constitution Party higher-ups, who stuck him with many of the party's outstanding financial obligations.

Grandfather and Grandmother, who was the soft-spoken opposite of the blustering General, came to visit us often in Winston-Salem.

When he was napping in an easy chair in our home one time, I thought he might appreciate a pillow to rest his head on. He did not, and he let fly with a stream of invectives directed at me, words I'd never heard at that volume level.

We saw them in Washington, D.C., at their apartment in the Kennedy-Warren building on Connecticut Avenue, next door to the entrance of the National Zoo where I visited Smokey Bear countless times.

By the time I, his young grandson, could converse with him, he was in the initial stages of Alzheimer's disease, and his behavior was beginning to become problematic for those around him.

One day, he got it in his head that my father would like a nice bottle of Southern Comfort, which could not have been further from the truth. As we drove by the ABC Store that was in Thruway Shopping Center, he tried to open the door of the moving vehicle to go shop for Dad's gift. I reached over and locked it. He blew a gasket and began yelling.

His advancing condition was undoubtedly harder on his wife and my mother than it was for me, but it became a huge problem one afternoon when I was 7.

Grandfather decided that he wanted to visit my mother who ran the "Pink Lady" gift shop she'd founded at the new Forsyth Memorial Hospital. We lived about five minutes away.

I sat in the passenger seat of his white Mercury Comet, and off we went. I remember nothing of the actual visit to Mom itself, but the ride home was memorable.

Grandfather wanted to get back on Interstate 40 from Silas Creek Parkway when we were leaving. I had yet to master the concepts of 'left' and 'right' and could only extrapolate to using 'east' and 'west' from having stared at maps in our antique encyclopedias.

When it came time to get onto I-40, I sent him the wrong way down an exit ramp, and we found ourselves driving into rush-hour traffic coming directly at us.

The General was furious and confused, shouting at me for what he perceived as my fault that we were going the opposite direction from all those other cars. He drove and hollered, and I cowered.

We were sideswiped by several of them until we veered into the median where local law authorities came to see what was going on. Nobody was injured, fortunately, but a few cars were damaged.

I was terrified, but probably more afraid of my oversized grandfather's bellowing accusations and recriminations about my sending him down the wrong side of the highway.

For many years, I took full (albeit silent) responsibility for having created the accident, despite still being years away from having a driver's license of my own. It undoubtedly precipitated a quicker mastering of "left" and "right" however.

But I never held it against my grandfather whose only fault that day was wanting to see his daughter at her work when he was in a compromised state. •

Copyright 2024, Peter Holsapple

Peter Holsapple grew up in Winston-Salem and now lives in Durham, North Carolina. Most of his life, Peter has spent time in the public eye as a songwriter and musician; but since his teenage years, he has toyed with the idea of writing prose. He is grateful to the PSPP for helping him to realize it is actually something he can do.

# On What Not To Do When Traveling
## by Mirinda Kossoff

Fresh from the Vienna Crime Museum, my 19-year-old twin sons and I were trapped in a parking garage in Vienna. I had parked there for the day while we visited the museum and other Viennese attractions—like the Opera House. You could say we went from the shifty to the sublime in one day.

The place was empty with no ticket booth nor anyone in sight to ask about how to exit.

I had ignored the German language sign at the lot entrance. Too bad I didn't speak German. Too bad for us.

"What are we going to do, Mom?" one of my sons asked.

"The only way I see is to tail the next car that leaves and follow close behind before the gate comes down."

"Oh, geez," Mom. "The gate could crash down on the roof of the car," said one. "Yeah," said the other, "that's not a great plan."

"Well, have you got any better ideas?" I said, acidly.

Silence.

I positioned our Peugeot to lie in wait for another auto to exit. Five minutes later, bingo! I nearly glued the Peugeot's front fender to the exiting car's rear bumper and skated through. I raised my fists in victory.

"Mom, put your hands back on the wheel," came the chorus who did not share my enthusiasm about the successful caper.

My pride was short-lived as I took a right turn out of the lot—onto the path of an oncoming trolley.

"Mom!"

I escaped a trolley collision by swiftly taking another turn off the tracks. "That was intense," I said.

With relief, I got the Peugeot on the road back to Prague, where we had started out.

Czech drivers were suicidal. They had a habit of passing a car with a car oncoming. Every one of my muscles was braced for a possible collision. My back was aching, so I saw a nice Viennese doctor who gave me some pain pills. "I'm driving," I explained, "so I don't want anything that will make me sleepy."

"You'll be fine," she reassured me.

I was not fine. On the freeway back to Prague, I fought the urge to nap and looked for an off-ramp to get some caffeine into my veins. The only off-ramps I saw went to nowhere. Both sons were blissfully napping.

The next thing I knew, my head bounced off the driver's side window, waking me with a start. During my involuntary nap,

I had struck a median. I looked to see if my sons were okay, and they both responded, "What happened?"

"I fell asleep at the wheel," I said, full of shame.

I got out to see the damage: Not bad but the median had put a hole in one tire so I couldn't drive back to the rental agency.

Mercifully, a cop car, looking more like a blue tinker toy with a round yellow flashing bulb on top, pulled up behind me. Two officers got out and approached me, speaking Czech. I pointed to the flat tire and made a motion I hoped would convey changing it. "Fix and back to rental agency," I said hopefully.

"Get in car," they said, pointing to the tinker toy. (*Did I mention that my sons are about 6'2"?*) The cops ushered us to the back seat of the two-door cop car, so we had to jackknife ourselves into the rear seat, stuffed in like tinned sardines.

When we arrived in the police station's parking lot, we unfolded our origami selves from the back seat to the front of a cement building reminiscent of Soviet-era construction. The cops led us through the door into a dingy room smelling of urine. A man behind a desk started typing up the accident report. "Drugs?" asked one officer.

"No." I wasn't about to tell them about the pain pills.

When the ancient typewriter finally coughed out the accident form, one cop said in English, "now you pay one hundred crowns."

I didn't have one hundred crowns. My money was in Austrian schillings (their currency before the Euro). I put the schillings

*On What Not To Do When Traveling*

on the countertop. No.

I put out a credit card. No. Of course they had no way to process it. The officer stood with arms crossed, unmoved.

One son piped up, "Mom, what's going to happen?"

"We have to pay this bribe, or they will keep us here until God knows when," I said through gritted teeth.

"I have fifty crowns from when we were in Prague," he offered.

"Give 'em to me."

Then I said brightly in the little German I knew, "*meine kinder hast* fifty crowns."

"Okay," said the officer, brightening. "Student fee."

We sat on the curb outside for the rental agent to fetch us. Lesson learned. •

Copyright 2024, Mirinda Kossoff

Mirinda Kossoff is the author of *The Rope of Life: A Memoir*, published in 2020. Her writing life has centered around journalism and creative nonfiction. She penned a weekly column for a local paper, was an essayist/commentator on regional public radio, and taught essay writing at Duke University in a continuing education program now called OLLI. She has been published in newspapers, national magazines, and in print and online literary journals.

# Roped In

by Alison Rice Bruster

I blame the debacle that followed on my roommate's decision to teach the class how to cut up a chicken.

It was the summer of 1982. Sherry and I were in our final semester at the University of Georgia. We had one last class to take before we claimed our college degrees. In the summer session, without the frenzy of Greek social activities and Bulldog football, life moved at a more languid pace. With just one class, we spent the bulk of our time hanging out at the campus swimming pool and enjoying our leisure.

We signed up for the Fundamentals of Public Speaking not because we were particularly interested in the subject, but because it sounded easy, and its 11 a.m. time slot meant we didn't have to get up early.

The class was focused on a series of speeches we had to write and deliver. Toward the end of the semester, the assignment was a demonstrative speech, teaching your audience how to do something by showing them how it's done. The professor told us he would give extra credit for the use of "creative visual aids."

This was the era when we learned to program computers by typing holes through punch cards and feeding them into a giant mainframe computer. The Internet, the iPhone, and Artificial Intelligence were still years away. So, the logical thing to do for this speech was to pick a subject we knew well and could easily demonstrate.

Sherry worked summers in a chicken processing plant near her home in North Georgia. She decided to teach the class how to cut up a chicken, something she had done many, many times. I can't remember what she used as her visual aid. Did she bring a raw chicken (and its attendant bacteria) into class and cut it up? She can't remember either, so the truth remains lost in the mists of time.

What I am sure about is that her speech was riveting. She had full command of the room as we learned a new skill from an expert in the trade. This left me pondering what I could do to match the dramatic effect. Her knife work was flashy; her execution, captivating.

And that's where things started to go off the rails.

Instead of speaking on a topic I knew something about, I came up with a brilliant plan that would guarantee extra credit for my visual aid. I was dating a guy named Jeff, whose hobbies included rock climbing. I asked him to teach me how to tie a climbing knot, and I borrowed one of his climbing ropes to serve as my visual aid. He schooled me on rock climbing, and I practiced tying the knot until it became second nature.

On the day I was to speak, I walked into class wearing a huge coil of climbing rope wrapped around my body, extending from my left shoulder to my right hip. When it was my turn, I strode to the front of the room and began my speech.

I talked breezily about rock climbing, the different kinds of knots you need, and the circumstances where you use them. Then, I took one end of the rope and confidently showed the class how to tie an Alpine Butterfly Loop to create a secure loop in the middle of the rope.

When I looked around the room, all eyes were glued to me. I could feel my energy rising as I brought my remarks to a close by encouraging them to get outside and give rock climbing a try.

The professor praised my speech and raved about my clever visual aid. I was flushed with pride. Then he asked for questions from the class.

And that's when it all came crashing down.

"How long have you been rock climbing?" An obvious query, given my apparent comfort with the topic, and I should have anticipated it.

I stood stunned and speechless for a moment, and then I heard a weak voice that sounded like mine, but from far away in a tunnel, say something stupid like "Uhm, well, I've NEVER been rock climbing, but my boyfriend climbs, and he taught me how to tie the knot." At this point, I would have welcomed

*Roped In*

a trap door underfoot to swallow me up, but no such luck. The exchange did shut down any more questions, though; the remaining raised hands lowered like balloons leaking helium. I slunk back to my seat as the next student stepped up.

In retrospect, I can see the trap I laid for myself. My speech and demonstration were skillful enough to convince the class that I was a rock climber, but my lack of foresight doomed me to flunk the Q&A. I sometimes wonder if I could have gotten away with it all if I were just a smoother, more confident liar. But then I should have known that things would not end well when I let a headless chicken lead me astray. •

Copyright 2024, Alison River Bruster

Alison Rice Bruster comes from a long line of women who love the written word. The granddaughter of a librarian, daughter of an English teacher, and sister of a novelist, she was destined to be an avid reader and writer. After a career spent finding the voices of senior business executives, she is writing a new chapter. She holds a BA in English Literature from Queens University of Charlotte and lives in Fort Mill, S.C. She is a member of the Charlotte Writers Club, Charlotte Lit, and the North Carolina Writers Network.

# Professor Curmudgeon
by Bob Amason

When I retired from the U.S. Air Force, I had the perfect job in mind: I would be a town curmudgeon. In my mind, this would involve finding a small southern town that lacked such a character and ensconcing myself in a rocker either on the porch of a feedstore or at the courthouse. There, I would "a'set eva' mornin', relaxin', rockin', and smokin' a seegar." People would come by and say, "Good mornin', Kunnel" (my exalted military rank). My true curmudgeonly reply would be, "It was a good mornin' 'til you got here!" Then, I would smile at my cleverness.

That would be my job. I reveled in that fantasy. I even had my eye on a white suit like Colonel Sanders wore. Everyone would know that I was really a tender-hearted soul, and the curmudgeonly comments were just a deflection from…well, from whatever people deflect from these days. Mothers would tell their impressionable little ones, "Don't mind him. He's just crotchety like that."

But 'twas not to happen. I got AFIB from the nitwit habit of smoking cigars and damn near died. That ruled out an essential element of "town curmudgeon." So, I became a college professor, the closest thing to a curmudgeon I could conjure up. I was a pretty good teacher, if I do say so myself, but I would have been an even better curmudgeon. *Damned cigars.*

At 53, I pursued a PhD in Higher Education Administration – I should be a college dean somewhere. The only problem with that vocation would be that after 22 years as a USAF officer, I was quite accustomed to asking someone to do something and knowing it would quickly get done.

Academe, on the other hand, is all about begging faculty members to consider the possibility of some new idea or other and hoping to see that idea come to fruition in the next 15-20 years. Faculty members are defined as "those who think otherwise." As an official curmudgeon, I would have been arrested by the campus police within hours of taking my first official university leadership position.

Oh, and I had some opportunities. I was at an insufferable cocktail party when the chancellor of one of America's state college systems asked me, "What do you want to do when you finish your degree?" I killed any chance of a job offer by growling, "Nothing. I think I'm going to move to the beach." Honest answer. The chancellor's eyes glazed over, and he stalked off. I had another sip of my scotch on the rocks and congratulated my curmudgeonly self for deflecting. It's what we curmudgeons do.

I finished that glass of spirits, had another, and contemplated my future. I decided that being a college professor has some curmudgeonly features all its own. You get to have sway in the classroom and fix your students with a beetle-browed visage, *a la* John Houseman in *The Paper Chase*. Haven't seen it? Great movie. Houseman, as Harvard Law Professor Charles Kingsfield, says to a student, "Mr. Hart, here's a dime. Call your mother and tell her there is serious doubt about you becoming a lawyer."

Man! What a great curmudgeon!

So that's what I did. I stayed a professor for 25 years.

It was a natural transition. I had already been a teacher since December 8, 1980. I know that date because it was the day I taught my first practice class at USAF Instructor Training. I was eating breakfast and contemplating my upcoming brilliant presentation in the classroom when the morning news announced that John Lennon had been shot in New York City. The day went sideways, and I don't remember the class I taught. Guess I did okay because I passed the course. It set me on the path I walked for over 40 years of teaching adults. I still miss John Lennon.

Later, as a dissertation chair, I learned I could get PhD students to do good research and write excellent dissertations by the mere threat of my John Housman-like curmudgeon jumping out. PhD students are uniformly desperate to satisfy their dissertation chairs. *Perfect!*

I chaired or participated in some 150 dissertation committees. I'm proud to say that my beetle-browed visage, combined with my intimidating growl, put the fear of God into about 150

PhD students over 15 years. Therefore, I helped birth some 150 new curmudgeons. At least, I hope they're curmudgeonly and insist on quality from their students. Our nation and the world need more hard-nosed researchers who insist on proof instead of opinion in solving intractable social problems.

I retired from teaching in 2021. Last week, I spotted an old-timey feedstore. It's less than a mile from my home. It might be a foolhardy move, but I'm looking for a white Colonel Sanders suit. •

Copyright 2024, Bob Amason

Award-winning author Bob Amason is a retired US Air Force Lieutenant Colonel and college professor. A Florida Writer's Association member, Bob writes under his pen name, Frank A. Mason. His *Journeyman Chronicles* series of American Revolutionary War novels are Amazon.com bestsellers. *Journeyman: Heart of Tempered Steel* won the 2023 Florida Writer's Association Gold Royal Palm Literary Award, Florida's most prestigious writing prize. Bob's writing has been published in four anthologies, academic journals, and books. He lives in Florida with his overachieving wife, a professor who is the author of a series of children's books.

# Here's a Deep Hole
## by Jim Riggs

Graduation week meant seniors finished classes three days early. On graduation day, Marlys and Adel joined Gaylen and me on our free afternoon paddling on Beaver Creek. My 15-foot Grumman was not quite enough canoe for four nearly grown young adults, but neither was my judgment good enough to match the self-confidence of youth.

Marlys' morning was spent at the beauty parlor. Adel's shorter hair took little maintenance. Gaylen and I had freshly trimmed flat-tops.

The girls wore shorts and neat blouses, the guys, swimming suits and white T-shirts. We were dressed for fun and sun on the water.

We enjoyed a wonderful afternoon paddling up and down the stream above the Beaver Creek dam.

Beaver Creek was relatively shallow. Marlys and Adel were non-swimmers, and I could tell by how tightly they held the thwarts, they were just a little nervous. I did not own a life jacket.

As I dragged my hand through the cool water, I answered their concern about the depth of the water by saying, "Here's a nice deep hole."

I handed my glasses to Adel. "Hold these please." Then I made a shallow dive out of the canoe into seven feet of water. As I hit the water, I glanced back over my shoulder. Behind me, like dancing dolls, my classmates twirled in three directions.

*Oh my God!* I thought. *What have I done?*

I swam toward my canoe, and somehow, lifted Adel into the water-filled canoe. I gave the boat a shove toward shore. It tipped again. Once more, I lifted her back into the canoe. This time I shoved it all the way into the muddy shore.

Marlys, still in seven feet of water, held Gaylen's head under water, screaming, "Oh my head! My head!"

*Oh no*, I thought. *She hit her head as the canoe flipped.*

I swam to Marlys and towed her into the mud along the shallow stream bank. Gaylen surfaced and I grabbed his hand, helping him join our bedraggled group of seniors. We were wet, cold, muddy, but alive. In a few hours we would walk across the stage and pick up our diplomas.

Marlys was unhappy. After three hours in the beauty shop, my graceful dive had ruined her hair. I soon learned that she had not injured her head as the canoe tipped. She had been holding Gaylen under water screaming, "Oh my hair! My hair!"

I offered to paddle the girls across the river to my car. Instead, they chose to wade through the calf-deep mud of a marsh toward Parkersburg.

Marlys never forgave me for ruining her hair. She had not a word to say to me at graduation that night. I only saw her once after that day when she came back for a class reunion. For her lifetime, she nurtured her hatred of me for ruining her hair on graduation day.

Later in the afternoon, I found Adel back at work at the variety store. We talked and laughed and celebrated being alive. Adel remained my friend, but I never again convinced her to go out with me.

The only casualties of our adventure were Marlys' hair and my glasses. In the confusion as the canoe tipped, Adel had dropped them.

So, at graduation, I missed the visual parts. We had a prayer and a speaker, and I received my diploma, but I have no idea what he talked about. *Can anybody remember?* He probably encouraged us to work hard, set worthy goals, and enjoy life. At the time, I was celebrating life but thinking about finding my glasses.

Three days later, on a warm, sunny, Sunday afternoon, I parked near the bank of Beaver Creek. I anchored my canoe near the spot where I came close to making graduation day a tragedy of stupidity. For an hour, I used my surface-diving skills to search the cold mud seven feet below the surface. A winter fish kill had left the bottom littered with carp bones that felt much like eyeglasses. Discouraged and chilled, I almost gave up when a set of fish bones came from my toes to my hands and morphed into a pair of taped-together, lime-coated spectacles. Neither I nor my family had money to replace my loss, so the astonishment at home at my finding them became a joyous celebration as a bit of vinegar cleared my foggy lenses.

Despite my ruined standing with Marlys and Adel, my relationship with Gaylen continued strong, even considering my ill-timed dive. We both spent the next year as freshmen at Iowa State College and our friendship—one might describe it as "deep"—has continued during our long lives. •

Copyright 2024, Jim Riggs

After a career teaching mathematics in Iowa, Jim retired to Hilton Head Island, South Carolina, where he loves exploring the beach and writing stories, both fiction and nonfiction. His first novel, Freedom Run drew rave reviews. He is presently working with other members of the Island Writers Network to tune up several others for publication, including his historical novel "Fannie" about his pioneer grandmother. His stories and poems have appeared in three anthologies from the Island Writers Network and the anthology *Twists and Turns* from the Personal Story Publishing Project.

# A Backward High
## by David Inserra

Standing in the shadow of the 30-foot-high Ferris wheel, my 8-year-old brain raced with anxious possibilities. The idea that the axle might disconnect filled me with dread. The massive metal wheel would spin across the field behind the school, crushing the Cotton Candy Shack, other rides, and the rows of tents filled with games of chance. Or maybe the workers would forget about me as my car dangled high atop the wheel. I would be stuck there, spending the rest of my life hovering over the Earth, wondering if I could ever make my way back down again.

I decided to stay on the ground and find other ways to be entertained unless I wanted to be the brunt of my brother's taunting.

Being two years older than me, my brother Steve always took care of me. If someone in school gave me a hard time, Steve would be there to stand up for his little brother and mess with the bullies if it did not stop.

The thing is, Steve thought he was the only one who had the right to give me the business. When we would charge through the woods, Steve would be the one to twist the pricker bush branch aside, causing it to fling back and whack me in the face. Often, when we would wrestle, Steve would ram me against the wall, where I would crumble to the ground, all the air knocked out of my lungs.

That was our relationship.

Steve sensed that I did not want to ride the Ferris wheel, so he called me scaredy pants. Mom and Dad put a quick stop to the teasing, but the damage was done. I did not like the idea of being twirled backward, making one rotation every twenty seconds or so. That, coupled with being dragged 30 feet into the air, filled me with a terror that I would never admit. I had to prove myself. So, I joined my brother in line, and a short time later, we climbed onto a long bench seat of the Ferris wheel car.

Mom and Dad stood to the side in the crowd and watched. Wide smiles across their faces. Dad's arm slipped around Mom's shoulder, and he pulled her tight.

As I sat there, ready to be launched into space, I thought of a plan. If I closed my eyes, I would not have to look at the specks of people milling about below us. The motion of the ride and the extraordinary heights would not cause my head to spin. I could enjoy this moment, and no one would ever know the dread that I felt. Or so I thought.

They secured all riders to make sure that they were not ejected from the seats as the operators spun them at high speeds through the sky. So, I grasped the safety bar. I sat tall. I threw my shoulders back and waited until we were locked in.

When I closed my eyes, it began. At first, simple sensations greeted me. The wheel moved, clicked, and stopped. Our car swayed. Below, giggling kids hopped on the ride. Then we moved again. Click, grind higher, and stop. One. Two. Three, I'm not really sure how many times this happened. Move, stop, and swing. Over and over. Then, the full spinning began. Continuous rolling. Round and round. With each rotation of the wheel, I felt my body being pulled backward, up, and high before it spun forward and plummeted. Then, the cycle continued. Maybe this went on for minutes—or hours. Maybe they could not stop the wheel, and we would be stuck spinning forever. I could not tell.

Then, the wheel abruptly stopped, and the car swayed. With my eyes closed, I could only guess what was happening. The cycle began again. Click. Grind. Spin. Sway. Movement. One car at a time must have been getting offloaded. It had to be. It was happening. Soon, I would be free.

The kids in the car below giggled while being offloaded. The attendant asked if they had a good time. With screams of joy, they shouted that they would do this again.

I opened my eyes. And then it happened. From deep inside, my stomach churned. I could not control the sensation. I leaned over the safety bar and let it go. An evening of snacks and sweets rained down upon the girls in front of the row waiting to board the ride.

*A Backward High*

My mom charged forward, ripping Kleenex out of her pocketbook, screaming that she was so sorry. My dad just walked away laughing. My brother pounded my arm, wondering why I would do such a thing.

As the attendant dragged me off the wheel, I staggered to my mom. My head still swam as she cleaned me up. Then I asked, "Can we get some funnel cake?" •

Copyright 2024, David Inserra

David Inserra lives on Hilton Head Island, South Carolina with his wife Ellen Titus and their dog, Mindy. David's most recent work appears in the PSPP release, Sooner or Later. He is a member of the Island Writers Network and works at the local Unitarian Church. David's first novel, a speculative thriller titled "In Your Own Backyard," is currently being queried to agents. He is also a musician who has written over 400 songs, most being about his wife. Visit davidinserra.weebly.com.

# Never Take a Snapping Turtle for a Ride

by Sondra Edwards

It was a typical April afternoon, with intermittent rain and sunshine and rainbows when my adventure began. My husband and I live on a farm just a few miles off the 194 Scenic Byway in Watauga County. At the time of this story, the acreage included two ponds stocked with beautiful speckled trout.

It was the end of my work week as a schoolteacher. As I headed home and turned into my driveway that day, I was stopped in my tracks by a huge snapping turtle strolling down the center of the lane. I had never seen a turtle so large! Its shell was at least 24 inches across. Its head, reminiscent of the alien in the movie ET, was surveying the driveway ahead. It was in no hurry. My car could not pass by it on either side. So, I just slowly followed as it meandered along. While in the car, I phoned my husband to say, "There is a sea turtle in our driveway!" He responded, "Do not let it get to the pond. It will eat our fish!" At that moment, the turtle sensed that it was being followed and began to amble into the tall grass on the left of the driveway, leaving just enough space for me to get past and continue to the house.

Quickly I parked the car. I looked back toward the pond and to my surprise, that turtle had quit meandering and was briskly heading toward the pond dam! I did not realize a turtle could sprint. Grabbing a snow shovel as a deterrent and an umbrella from the garage (because another April shower had begun), I raced to the pond dam to thwart the turtle's efforts to feast on our fish. Thus, my Ninja Turtle dance began in the pouring rain, my umbrella in one hand and the shovel in the other. I matched wits with Mr. Turtle seemingly for an eternity. Each direction he turned, the blade of a snow shovel blocked his path. At this point, I learned that a pissed-off turtle can hiss very loudly.

At last, my husband arrived in his truck. He took the shovel and held it at an angle and the turtle bit down on the edge of it so strongly that my husband was able to hoist it into the truck bed. There he lay, all 50 pounds of him, staring at us.

Now what? We had accepted an invitation to a dinner party and had no time at the moment to herd this turtle. Okay, he will have to ride with us and maybe we can find another home for him after dinner.

We cleared the edge of town and were traveling at the speed limit down Highway 421, when I looked in the passenger rearview mirror and saw the turtle standing on its hind legs clinging to the side of the truck bed with its long claws. I shouted to my husband, "Can that turtle jump out of this truck?" Before he could answer, it leaped over the edge onto the shoulder of the highway! Landing upside down, it skidded on its shell several hundred feet before we could pull over and stop. We backed up to where it landed and noted it was still alive and even angrier, so it was easy to get it to bite the shovel again and repeat the scenario of tossing it back into the truck bed.

On we went to the dinner party hosted by a family who owned sheep. While we were enjoying our meal, we told the story. The host suggested, "Let's go see that turtle." Lo and behold, it was not in the truck bed. It had once again jumped from the truck and was now climbing up the hill toward the pasture of sheep. The host shrieked, "A turtle that big can break a sheep's leg." He ran to his garage and came back with a huge trash can. He and my husband maneuvered the turtle into the trash can, set the can in the back of the truck, and snapped on the lid. After dinner, we took a detour to a bridge over in the next county. At approximately 9 p.m. in the dark of that evening, after experiencing quite a harrowing day, my husband and I released Mr. Turtle from the trash can at the bridge and with a huge splash he became a resident of Ashe County and fodder for a memorable family story.

Many months later, my husband was enjoying breakfast with some guys who like to get together to tell lies. One man said, "One day I was riding down 421 and I saw a turtle jump out of a truck!"

"Yeah?" my husband declared. "Well, I was driving that truck!" •

Copyright 2024, Sondra Edwards

Sondra Edwards, wife, mother of two, grandmother of five, children's minister, and music educator, lives in the mountains of Boone, North Carolina. Now retired, she dabbles in visual arts and creative writing. For the past four years, she has participated in the writing group of Sue Spirit. More recently, she joined a community writing group led by Joseph Bathanti, former NC Poet Laureate and Appalachian State University professor. She is the author of *The Innkeeper's Feast*, a Christmas pageant based on the model of a Madrigal Feast. The play is published by Leader Resources.

# Accidental Degrees and Grandmother Time
## by Susie Wilde

I got my first ticket for a moving violation when I was rushing home from my mother's dementia facility to avoid five o'clock traffic. It was a spot where the speed limit changed quickly, and the warning signs were few. I paid my fine, and my record was expunged.

Two months later, while dashing across town to deliver the new clothes my mother's caretakers had requested, I got a second speeding ticket. This one was issued in front of the elementary school my children had attended. I knew the school was far from the scene of my crime and 15 minutes later the speed limits changed, but I obsessed on how I could have caused a child's death.

Before that, I'd prided myself on the fact that I could do more than anyone I knew in 24 hours. Being in a hurry worked well for me, or I thought it had. But that second ticket proved that stuffing my days full to bursting could be dangerous. "Now," my husband joked, "you'll be the only one in our family with a graduate degree in driving."

I wasn't laughing. "Ron," I told him, "I'm going to give you veto power over my life." After complaining for years about how he tried to control me, I was giving him sway over my decisions. Every morning for several months, we met to scale down my errands until they were reasonable. "Today, I'm taking my mom to the dentist," I'd begin, "On the way, I can drop off my old clothes at the Thrift Store and zip into a store to get jars for making peach jam."

"Do one, not both," Ron suggested. On the way to pick up my mom, I held tight to the steering wheel, putting brakes on my compulsion as I passed the store where canning jars lived.

Trimming errands did not work the evening I dashed out to visit my mother one last time before I left to work in Wales for several weeks. I collected my third ticket for tailgating a marked highway patrol car. His brake lights glowed red in the fading sunset as he warned me, gently, to slow down. My focus was on reaching my mother, so I continued to follow him too closely until he pulled me over.

Working in Cardiff freed me from driving and from potential police stops. On my last day in Wales, I went to a psychic and asked how I might retain some of the peace I'd recently found. "You need to hold the hand of Grandmother Time," she told me. I researched Native American figures, read up on Norse gods, scanned Greek myths but found no such person. Back in North Carolina, curiosity took a back seat to catch-ups and to-dos, including scheduling traffic school.

That first week home I visited my mom's residency daily, savoring sauntering through the facility's corridors as I sang with her. It was a ritual we had begun when she was beyond holding a conversation and reading aloud no longer held her interest. My mother proved that music is stored in a special part of the brain as her musical memory of the silly songs she'd taught me as a child had endured beyond most things she'd lost. In the excellent reverb of my mother's lockdown unit, I relaxed into our steady pacing, appreciating how our notes rang out as we sang indelicate songs like "Rosabelle McGee who tipped the scales at 303" and Ann Boleyn who "walked the bloody tower with her head tucked underneath her arm."

I realized the sun was casting shadows in the parking lot and I still had dinner to prepare. "Mama," I said, "I have to go." We sang as we walked to the locked door that separated my mother from the world. At my car, I turned to wave, and she raised her arm in response. The fading sun lit her silvering hair, and I understood the mystery I'd carried home from Wales.

"Grandmother Time" was my mother.

My three tickets, each more dramatic than the one before, warned me to slow down, that speeding through life was not the way to care for my mother or myself. She had always known how to rest, and our singing walks created the pause I seemed unable to give myself at any other time. After holding her hand and singing, I always breathed more deeply, more slowly. As I drove home, my attention mostly on the road, I realized I had discovered a path to peace, preferrable to the one leading to a PhD in driving. •

Copyright 2024, Susie Wilde

Susie Wilde wrote reviews and interviews in columns and articles for newspapers and magazines countrywide for 40 years. Her longer published works include a picture book, *Extraordinary Chester*, and *Write-A-Thon! How to Conduct a Writing Marathon in Your Class*. She teaches, influences, and works on her memoirs. Discover more at her website: www.ignitingwriting.com

# Just One More Thing
by Randell Jones

I drive a lot. I'm a "road warrior" in the minds of some. I'd rather drive than fly.

In all that driving, I see plenty of ad hoc memorials placed alongside roadways, tributes to a loved one lost at that spot. Someone who expected to greet another day never got that chance. Tragedy struck instead. I remember too many times—by my own recklessness—I tempted fate. But good fortune, luck of the Irish, or the hand of God, for reasons not known, said, "Not yet."

During my college days at Georgia Tech, we were InCel before that was a thing—"involuntarily celibate." Our student body of 5,000 had only 50 women, as far as anyone knew. But the "Law of the Duck"—looks like/walks like—persuaded us. Chances were none of us would ever know for sure.

Instead, during those days at Tech, I was trying to solve, along with differential equations and integral calculus, the mysteries of life with the help of some like-minded fellows in a social fraternity. Our Greek tribe provided a social outlet, a place to party, to drink underage, and to be around college-age women imported from God knows where.

Not surprising in this Land of the Nerds, I was a dateless wonder that fall 1968, so I occupied myself otherwise. I'd been awake for 36 hours. I was a pledge, helping with the Homecoming display out front and then keeping the mechanically inclined company while they tinkered out back with our entry into the Ramblin' Wreck Parade. So, on Saturday afternoon when a fraternity brother asked me if I'd take his date for the rest of the day, it was an offer too good to pass up.

She was his blind date, one of the imports from Mercer College in Macon. He and she had been to the football game at midday but did not hit it off. She and somebody else's date had come up for the day and would get a ride home after the party. So, sleep-deprived or not, I would have a date that evening for the dancing and drinking and whatever else I could finagle at a time when rowdiness consisted of the brothers and their dates standing in a circle when the band took a break and singing bawdy songs with tongue twisters revealing how drunk our dates were. It was obnoxious and disrespectful but relatively tame by any comparison with misogyny today. It was a game both genders played in those days before women's liberation improved the lot for my own daughters' world, better but not perfect.

I don't remember her name, nor she mine, I'm sure. But it was Homecoming and we made the best of the evening, dancing and drinking enough to smash down our late-adolescent insecurities in a contest to elevate ourselves above our worst fears about our lovability. And then it was time to take her back to Mercer. *Jesus, that was 90 miles. Road trip!*

We got to the dorms at Mercer and dropped off the young women, they happier than anyone to end the day. Then we headed home. No interstate highways then, at least not completed all the way. We were on some two-lane road at 2 a.m., headed north, just me and the guy who had the car and the other date. I was along for the ride and glad for a chance to sleep. I'd soon be seeing my third dawn in a row without so much as a nap.

I could hardly hold my head up. Which is why I was so surprised to awaken with my head resting on the passenger window from exhausted sleep for no apparent reason except to see we were driving up hill on the wrong side of the road and the driver's chin was on his chest. I yelled, "Hey, Brad!" His head jerked up and he swerved back into the right lane just as we crested the hill, and an 18-wheeler blew past us in a rush.

I don't know why I woke up. Should not have. Had no reason to surface from such a deep slumber to prevent myself and the driver from becoming two greasy spots on the highway and just another story that would be forgotten soon after the makeshift crosses and the plastic flowers disappeared from the side of the road.

Whether saved by my Irish luck, good fortune, or the hand of God, I am grateful, for that and a few other instances over the half century since that have no explanation for my survival except grace. I don't take it for granted. No longer uncertain about my lovability, I hope I've lived a life worth saving. And also, I deeply hope the universe has at least one more reason for me being here a little bit longer, something I am yet supposed to do.

Yeah, please, at least, just one more thing. •

Copyright 2024, Randell Jones

Randell Jones is an award-winning writer about the pioneer and Revolutionary War eras and North Carolina history. During 25 years, he has written 150+ history-based guest columns for the Winston-Salem Journal. His newest release is the expanded 2nd edition of the 2005 biography and travel guide, *In the Footsteps of Daniel Boone* (2024). In 2017, he created the Personal Story Publishing Project and in 2019, the companion podcast, "6-minute Stories" to encourage other writers. He lives in Winston-Salem, North Carolina.
Visit RandellJones.com and BecomingAmerica250.com.

www.ingramcontent.com/pod-product-compliance
Lightning Source LLC
Chambersburg PA
CBHW020232170426
43201CB00007B/402